A GUIDE FOR THERAPISTS AND PATIENTS TO SHORT-TERM PSYCHOTHERAPY

A GUIDE FOR THERAPISTS AND PATIENTS TO SHORT-TERM PSYCHOTHERAPY

By

E. LAKIN PHILLIPS, Ph.D.

Professor of Psychology
Director of the Counseling Center
The George Washington University
Washington, D.C.

CHARLES C THOMAS • PUBLISHER
Springfield • Illinois • U.S.A.

Published and Distributed Throughout the World by

CHARLES C THOMAS • PUBLISHER
2600 South First Street
Springfield, Illinois 62717

ISBN 0-398-05130-5

Library of Congress Catalog Card Number: 85-2705

With THOMAS BOOKS *careful attention is given to all details of manufacturing and design. It is the Publisher's desire to present books that are satisfactory as to their physical qualities and artistic possibilities and appropriate for their particular use.* THOMAS BOOKS *will be true to those laws of quality that assure a good name and good will.*

Printed in the United States of America
Q-R-3

Library of Congress Cataloging in Publication Data

Phillips, E. Lakin (Ewing Lakin), 1915-
A guide for therapists and patients to short-term psychotherapy.

Includes bibliographies and index.
1. Psychotherapy, Brief. I. Title.
[DNLM: 1. Psychotherapy, Brief. WM 420 P558g]
RC480.55.P48 1985 616.89'14 85-2705
ISBN 0-398-05130-5

INTRODUCTION – SOMEWHAT AUTOBIOGRAPHICAL COMMENTS

SHORT-TERM psychotherapy is here to stay!

In fact, it's been here for a long, long time – and you see it clearly when you get down to the facts – but if you pay attention only to the official literature and the public stereotypes, you will miss the practicalities and think therapy is only a long-term, prodigious, expensive, onerous process. Nothing could be more distant from the facts.

Throughout the U.S.A. there are over 600 community mental health clinics, supported partly by federal funds, partly by local and state funds. (There are still other clinics privately or locally supported.) Over a 9-year period, from 1970 to 1978, about 45 to 50 million (yes, *million*) persons – individuals, groups, families – received psychotherapy in these settings.[1] This setting – the community mental health centers/clinics – is the backbone of all psychotherapy conducted in the country, a baseline so robust it cannot be gainsaid.

The average number of therapy sessions for these 45 to 50 million cases (persons) was a little over 5 sessions, covering a 9-year period! Take this report as a contrast to the following one.

When I came to Washington, D.C. in 1948 to teach at The George Washington University, I also studied at the Washington School of Psychiatry and underwent an analysis there, as part of my training but also for personal reasons. At the same time, I worked at the Arlington (Va.) County Health Department as a clinical psychologist, working with a staff of 8 to 10 psychiatrists, social workers, and an occasional other psychologist. All of them were in training and analysis at the Washington School of Psychiatry, since that was the best place to study and be analyzed, following the "interpersonal relations" viewpoint laid down by Harry Stack Sullivan. Even though Sullivan was heralded as one who had broken from Freudian notions to a considerable extent, it was soon evident that the "break" was more in name than fact. People were in analysis for hundreds of hours, spending, I suppose, a goodly part of their earnings for this treatment in the hopes of better lives and better professional preparation. It was an extant notion then that one serious about clinical work should belong to "the thousand hour club," meaning, of course, that one should be really thoroughly analyzed — whatever *that* meant — and wear the badge of approval (1000 hours of therapy) by one's knowledgeable and powerful peers.

I was brought up on this general viewpoint during my fledging years as a psychotherapist and accepted it to a limited degree. My early teaching experiences at the University of Minnesota, when a student there, at Macalaster College in St. Paul, Minnesota during the early postwar years when I was finishing my graduate work at the University began to open my eyes somewhat. After the war (1946-1948) I picked up loose ends and finished my training and research and worked some in local psychological clinics at the St. Paul and Minneapolis Public Schools.

The University of Minnesota has always been known as the center of "dust bowl empiricism" a reputation rightly deserved. I had been trained to appreciate and seek out hard facts, a matter highly compatible with my small town, semirural Missouri upbringing; so I was quite at home with the Minnesota viewpoint. However, in Washington, D.C. I soon came to realize that there was a profound and ranging difference between my University of Minnesota scientific upbringing on the one hand and my newly encountered experiences at the Washington School of Psychiatry, the Arlington Clinic (my clinical contacts there with patients and with peers), and in relation to, and contrast with, my analysis, on the other hand. I was immersed into the clinical world of Washington, D.C. — a community already strongly influenced by the Washington-Baltimore Psychoanalytic Society and the whole Eastern seaboard predelictions for psychoanalysis, from Boston to Miami — and I began to experience the pain arising from the discrepancies with my earlier training. How was I to survive this dilemma, progress scientifically and clinically, keep my sanity and maintain peer relationships in some semblance of order and respectability?

In a while I began to realize that in Washington, D.C. I had become part of a tremendous overlay of theory and speculation that had very little substance. I knew friends and patients who had had years and years and hundreds of hours, maybe even thousands of hours, of psychoanalysis, and appeared no different as far as I could tell from what they were like before they embarked on this journey into self-examination. I also observed at the Arlington County Mental Health Center that patients — individuals, families, groups — did fairly well in a few sessions.[2] I also observed — and did a little research on the topic (which was the background in the more recent interests in attrition from psychotherapy) — that very few patients stayed in therapy very long. Did they get something, nonetheless? I was not then aware of the large scale attrition issues involved — clinically, statistically, cost-wise — as I have come to be since, but I had the embryonic basis laid for my later skepticism, research, and writing, of which this book is partly a culmination and distillation.

Among the persons I knew fairly well who had hundreds of hours of psychoanalysis and evidenced no clearcut improvements, I recall conversations with many who said that while they did not experience much symptom (or manifest) change, they felt they understood themselves better as a result of the extensive treatment (and thousands of dollars outlay).

I plodded along with my teaching, beginning research and student contacts at George Washington University, all the while going to classes and seminars at the Washington School of Psychiatry and engaging in psychoanalysis (modified, I suppose, as I went only 2 to 3 times a week for several years, a paltry regimen compared to some who were — and had been — going 4, 5, 6 times a week for years). Looking back on my work at the Washington School of Psychiatry I now believe my best and most thought-provoking training came from courses I had with socially-oriented theorists and practitioners. I saw very little relationship between the clinical theories and the social theories, except in the broadest of outlines; nothing of a social, theoretical, or research nature ever seemed to stimulate change at the *clinical* level, and the talk about clinical differences — as between Freud and Sullivan, Horney and Freud, Fromm and Freud, and so on — never held up in any research or demonstrable way that made any impact on anything people were doing. Lots of talk and no action!

While I was engaged in all of the above, I did some consulting with preschools in the nearby Virginia and Maryland suburbs. There I interacted with parents, teachers, and, of course, the little ones. The children presented the usual range of problems: aggression toward one another for privilege, possessions, attention; reluctance to follow the teacher's regimen; sulking; dependence upon parents and thus some unwillingness to get into the swim of things at the preschools; and, of course, the ubitiquous problems of urinary self-control and continence. We grappled with these issues weekly in visits I made to the preschools, in evening meetings with parents (usually mothers but some fathers now and then), and in arranging matters of routine at the preschool itself so as to bring out the best — and minimize the worst — in children. All of that experience taught me to respect the social environment, the interpersonal relationships, although I had no well-defined conceptual ways of arranging these experiences succinctly and economically. Freud was of no use, I was beginning to realize; Rogers was helpful but in very limited ways; and behaviorism in the sense of Skinner's ideas applicable to clinical work had not yet been actuated. Behaviorism appeared more clear in the late 1950s with Skinner's work and with related work by Eysenck and a scattered number of others.[3]

I had already anticipated in my own way some of the behavioral movement: I recommended to the preschool parents and teachers that they not respond, cajole, exhort the children who were "naughty" or oppositional, but rather to let them "spend" their protests without definitive response other than minimizing or ignoring them. (I got more flack from both parents and teachers about this viewpoint, because they alleged I was ignoring an important "need," else the matter would not have occurred so vehemently and/or so often among the children). Nonetheless, I answered the parents and teachers — the more important matter was the child's behavior changing for the better, and evidence mounted that was, indeed, the case. The behavioral movement came to call this "time out," meaning, of course, "time out from positive reinforcement," which, further, meant that if you belabored the issues with the child you, as teacher or parent, were acknowledging the importance of the issue (reinforcement through attention) and were therefore weakening your ability to influence the child otherwise and strengthening the child's unwanted behavior, I also recommended children be placed away from the mix among the others until the offending (disturbed, momentarily unhappy child) realized his/her kicks were with the others and not with making one-person stands for attention, control, and the like. This, too, was part of the time-out measure. I once had an architect as a client (concerning his children), and I discussed with him the advisability and practicality of having small areas or carrels built into schools as havens for the distressed child so they could unobtrusively and momentarily be placed away from the group; and, additionally, as potential encouragement for the child to earn the right to get back into the mix through better self-control, all without admonishment from the adults, I should add.

What did all this teach me? It taught me that people are people, sharing personality characteristics and everything else, as they interact with others. One does not come to school, or work, or marriage, or anything with wholly encrusted tendencies (although there are, of course, physiological, neuroanatomical, structural limits on what we can or cannot do, such as how fast we can run). How one acts in a given set of circumstances points a clear finger to the interpersonal influences afoot at the time; otherwise one would be the same in and under all circumstances. Working with families also taught me more about how these conflicts work in the home, between parents, and how the child mirrors conflicts — serious or not — between the parents. Also, how each parent on different occasions could vary in behavior toward the child (made possible by inconsistencies derived from fatigue, distractions, anger at being confronted, and so on). I substituted the familiar, "tender, loving care," with "firmness, fairness, and consistency," meaning that the latter would give rise to the former, and that you should not pursue the former in the absence of the latter.[4]

From children and families I moved toward work with college students when I became director of the George Washington University Counseling Center in 1962 along with a dual appointment as professor of psychology. This was the beginning of my more concerted work on psychotherapy (although I had published in 1956 my first thoughts and viewpoints about psychotherapy, arising as I have said above, from my own analysis, from my studies and teaching, and from my experiences with children, families, groups, adolescents, and adults).[5] (All of the latter clients appeared regularly under my service as I worked in the Arlington County (Va.) Mental Health Center.)

Why this autobiographic excursion? It is to allow the reader to see that I have come to my ideas, research and practices written about herein, forged on the anvil of experience, tempered with research, and coated with endless discussions with my students, colleagues, clients, and, of course, with those who read my writings and reacted both positively and negatively to them. I now believe that we stand at a huge crossroads concerning the practice of psychotherapy (and counseling, since this term overlaps somewhat with psychotherapy, but more often has its applications in strictly educational settings where courses, careers, etc. are the uppermost problems presented by people rather than so-called personal/social/emotional problems). The crossroads say whether we should pursue psychotherapy and behavior change from the traditional standpoint, the "depth" model promulgated by Freud and followed in the Western world by most psychotherapists until recently; or whether we should look to what we actually do — the actual record of clients of therapists working in clinics. Should we not extract from them the best and most parsimonious things we already do, but need to upgrade? We need to emphasize the latter, I think, because that is the only way to "do psychotherapy," and meet consumer needs. And it is the only justifiable way in a practical, research, and training sense as well. To believe in a depth model but to practice a social model is to be inconsistent, inefficient and to even confuse the client beyond what is already naturally present in any self-change process.[6]

This book is an effort to bring forth considerations for therapist and client alike, considerations that are the most efficacious or promising for all concerned. The therapist will get more kicks practicing short-term therapy because s/he is helping more people and that is a good and rewarding thing. The clients and the public will come to see that a short time in therapy, if it is needed at all, will bring a modicum of practical benefits (if it is well-conducted) for most people. These benefits, while they may need upgrading and bolstering now and again, will serve them well.

I am proud to say that I sometimes get calls from former clients seen anywhere from ten to twenty or twenty-five years earlier. They remind me that they had a good encounter then and wonder if I remember them (or their children) and would I be willing to see them again for a short spell to go over a current problem. Since I have never advertised my practice — never, in over 35 years had my name in the yellow pages of any phone book, although I am listed in professional directories, in local and national registers — I have drawn clientele almost entirely by personal recommendations and by word-of-mouth. Usually when the former client returns, it is for a very brief spell, although, to be sure, there are exceptions. I have only a few times seen patients more than one time a week, seldom two, and never three times a week. I have allowed clients to call me for good and ample reasons between sessions if there was a particularly difficult or crisis-ridden situation confronting them (analysts would usually abhor this practice); but seldom has this privilege been abused, and never for longer than it took me to wise up and bring it to a halt.

This book, then, covers the most salient issues in short-term therapy. Some have arisen in my personal experience, some in the vast literature on therapy. I will not burden the reader with interrupting references to research or the writing of others, saving that for the end of the book (for the interested reader, client, or therapist). The book is intended – Mr./Ms. therapist, Mr./Ms. client – to help you think more clearly about the therapy enterprise and to see its benefits and limitations in clear light. I do not think therapy will cure all ills, nor do I think everyone should have therapy. Therapy should be used with reasonable discretion and, at first, tentatively; more therapy, if really needed, of course, but not more just because more is available. In the literature on therapy, a significant number of people – as has already been indicated – come for a few sessions, and many return for another – or, perhaps, still another – few sessions. The idea of an exhaustive, almost interminable, "thorough" analysis of all of one's life is not only impossible, it would be highly distracting, disadvantageous, and far too costly. Even the few who can so indulge themselves cannot be counted among the most successful cases. A little bit of judicious help is the hallmark of wise counsel, be it psychotherapy, advice from a lawyer, a physician or your preacher, priest, or rabbi.

And one last point: If you consult the professional literature on psychology on popular mental hygiene books, on psychotherapy and personal growth and adjustment, etc., you will see that most such books are more opinion than fact. Not often, and not to a very great degree do authors back up their assertions. In this book, I want to be careful on this point. Everything I say herein is at least indirectly supported by facts. That does not mean that facts are the end-all and be-all or that no argument can possibly exist. It does mean that I try to respond to, and include, facts as the basis for what I say, If I am unsure, I'll say so; if the scientific picture is blurred, and I know it, I'll report it. Let us now get on with the real values associated with short-term psychotherapy.

ACKNOWLEDGMENTS

ONE IS INDEBTED to many people when writing a book. I cannot name all who have my high regard for their help to me. But the staff at the George Washington University Counseling Center are among those I am most indebted to. My clients have been sources of inspiration, frustration, guidance and reinforcement; without them I would have nothing to say. My secretary, May Nakamura, has been a faithful, devoted, and indefatigable worker who has not only done a yoeman's job in typing and computer-assisted work, but also has offered excellent editorial assistance. Roslyn Tobin has also been of inestimable assistance at crucial times in the closing out of this work. I shall be very pleased if those who have stimulated me and taught me will, also, be rewarded by seeing this completed work.

CONTENTS

A GUIDE FOR THERAPISTS AND PATIENTS TO SHORT-TERM PSYCHOTHERAPY

Chapter 1

WHAT HAVE OTHERS SAID OF SHORT-TERM PSYCHOTHERAPY?

AS EVERYONE KNOWS, short-term psychotherapy has been around a considerable length of time.[1] It was even practiced by Freud, who at first, at least, held his analysis to about 6 to 12 months, albeit at a rate of several times a week. Rogers, too, began with a short-term emphasis, although it came out that more from his general viewpoint than an attempt to be short-term, per se. He noted, however, that as practiced over time, he and his followers gradually moved to longer-term therapy, but not of the interminable sort.[2]

Some of Freud's followers recommended short-term therapy and, moreover, to insure brevity, recommended time-limited therapy (which, by definition, is short-term: usually 10 to 20 sessions, or thereabouts). Adler wrote about time-limited therapy and practiced it; some of his followers did useful and pointed research on the matter of time-limited therapy.[3] It is a matter of agreeing at the outset that one has limited time, therefore limited goals. The issues at hand are first to decide what is most important; second, to structure problems in these areas; and third, proceed to mobilize efforts and pursue goals in therapy accordingly.

Another practice, besides time-limiting in advance that shortens therapy, is to have a set of prescriptions, efforts, purposes, expressed clearly so that one mobilizes his/her energies accordingly. As an example, one client indicated he was likely to be moved on his job in 6 months; he had that amount of time to decide if he was going to "keep his marriage" and expect his wife to go with him to the new job setting, or yield to her slight preference to stay in the area and with her job, letting her husband move and thereby dissolve the marriage. While the man posed the question in terms of these task and time limits, the wife went along with the order; she was involved secondarily in the husband's quest for a decision, although she preferred to have him stay with her, keep his regular job, and try to reconstitute the marriage.

A third factor that may limit time in therapy is money. Some insurance carriers place a 10, 20, 30, 50-session time limit on the amount of therapy they will support. Since therapy is often expensive, most people want insurance support and, indeed, pay for it in payroll deductions along with other medically-related expenses. Most people who accept this limitation are prepared at the outset to engage in therapy only a limited amount of time and they set their sights accordingly.

Therapy may also be time-limited in school and work settings. The end of the semester or the school year may set a very natural time limit on therapy, just as it does on student jobs, earning credits, preparing for graduation, a school transfer, another school, or all of these. In work settings, people often move from one place to another, or from one community to another, the limits imposed therewith setting limits also on therapy, especially if one wishes to work with a particular therapist and/or clinic before the move. All of life's events are more or less structured, time-limited, and these boundaries influence a large number of other activities, perhaps every aspect of one's living. Time limits then — despite our protests against being slavishly controlled by the clock and the calendar — are ever present, whether we like it or not. In most cases these limits are salutary; they may even be highly motivational, as we "get on the stick" when we know we have only a short while to accomplish something.

Presumably the best reason for limiting therapy time is because it is a salutary thing to do, irrespective of — or along with — natural time limits. Whenever something appears open-ended as to time, it tends to lull us into inactivity, encourage postponement, wastefulness. We know, too, in our personal lives, if we act to get the car fixed, the laundry done, the bank account adjusted, the phone calls made, we feel much better about these matters and ourselves. On the other hand, to indulge ourselves excessively leads to feelings of self-abnegation, low esteem, and embarrassment, even guilt. The popular literature of the masses over the ages attests to the "Get-It-Done-Now" philosophy.[4] That does not mean that we should not ponder things, or do our chores impulsively; it means once we know they must be done — due, often, to outside circumstances beyond our control — it is best to be dispatchful.

SOME VIEWS ON SHORT-TERM THERAPY

Dr. Jerome Frank did 25 years of research on short-term psychotherapy.[5] He concluded that what's important in short-term therapy are matters related to activating, testing out and confirming one's expectations; and, secondly, the learning of needed social skills. Those objectives look like ones to be achieved in fairly short order although, of course, one can go on improving on them as one can with his/her painting, singing, car repairing, cooking, and so on. The notion of great depth in the undertaking is clearly missing in the Frank account of short-term therapy. Frank also believed that the purpose and accomplishments of all therapy (satisfactory or not) was to help the person over depressive, self-demoralizing, self-abnegating feelings. To self-generate for future decisions and accomplishments is a desired outcome from psychotherapy, according to Frank.

Another researcher/practitioner of short-term therapy is Wells.[6] He states that psychotherapeutic intervention operates early on in the process; after a good start the person — and nature — tend to take over and the person learns to "go it on his own." Wells also says (p. 23), "Short-term treatment should be considered the treatment of choice in such settings as mental health clinics and child guidance and family service agencies except where there is specific empirical evidence that a particular client group or presenting problem requires lengthier treatment." Apropos of both short-term psychotherapy and *planned* (short-term) psychotherapy, Budman says: "What is probably exceptional, however [in brief therapy] is *planned* brief therapy, that is treatment which is organized in such a way as to be maximally beneficial in a brief period (p. 463).[7] This quote, it is readily recognized, covers some of the points cited above as to how one takes advantage of natural time limits and then plans brief (or short-term) therapy.

Although talking about short-term dynamic psychotherapy (i.e., following essentially the Freudian model), Sifneos remarks that short-term therapy (perhaps in any of a number of forms) is here to stay and that it minimizes the various features of traditional analysis (holding transference to be more or less immutable, believing that research and study of therapy would injure the process, and that departure from rigid Freudian orthodoxy would not be good for the patient).[8] Actually, Sifneos feels that adherence to the orthodoxy is, itself, inimical to clients getting ahold of themselves, thereby seeming to make necessary lengthy therapy. Sifneos represents, among others, departure of a more or less extensive amount, from traditional, orthodox Freudian notions and practices. However, Sifneos still holds to some of the structural aspects of psychoanalytic practice (e.g., transference).

The opposite to short-term therapy is, of course, long-term therapy, either traditional Freudian psychoanalysis or "modified," or psychodynamic psychotherapy, holding as it does to some Freudian tenets, but reducing them in importance and stringency, or leaving some behind. In discussing rationale for short-term therapy, Malan[9] has asked why psychoanalysis changed from a briefer therapy in the first place; to which he suggests the following answers (paraphrased):

1. The notion of "resistance" has been overplayed, seen as a bulwark against change rather than as a matter requiring therapist skill in bringing the client to considering the most salient issues in his/her life encouraging change.

2. The notion of "overdetermination," which refers to the hardening of maladaptive (or "neurotic") tendencies, a kind of pathological "overkill" that is hard to overcome.
3. Considering what is called "working through" a necessary prerequisite to change meaning reliving, reexperiencing the allegedly traumatic events that started the person off in the present neurotic course.
4. Considering the basis of neurosis in the person's childhood, plus the necessity to exhume these origins.
5. Transference, where the client relives and sort of reassigns his/her difficulties to the therapist; a condition which then has to be analyzed.
6. Dependency. Simply, too much reliance on the therapist; too little self-instigation toward change.
7. Negative transference. This arises at the point of termination, allegedly, as the client does not want to let go and become independent.
8. The transference neurosis itself.
9. Therapist passivity toward the client, letting the latter lead when the client is, likewise, expecting direction.
10. The therapist conveying a sense of timelessness to the client; this is, of course, confused with salience, structure, getting on with the task.
11. Therapeutic perfectionism; meaning every last bit of problem has to be analyzed.
12. Going further and further back into one's past, one's feelings, etc.

While these are somewhat paraphrased, from Malan, they do cover the waterfront of traditional thinking in psychoanalysis, especially over the past 4 to 5 decades. This list from Malan contrasts sharply with present day practices of a short-term nature, whether among psychodynamically-oriented psychotherapists (such as Malan), or among eclectic or behaviorally-oriented therapists. In contrast to the above, note the following emphasis cited as characteristic of behavioral short-term psychotherapy (which is more explicit in its assumptions than eclectic, Rogerian or other forms of short-term therapy); from Wilson (paraphrased):[10]

1. Goals are limited; chosen by client and therapist; usually the client begins with "presenting complaints" and these, along with others that develop, are woven into more succinct and salient problem statements.
2. Therapy is focused on these named problems, and the feedback resulting from working on them.
3. Each therapy hour is so focused, present-time-centered, taking into account how the client feels about change, what is working and what is not working as well.
4. The therapist is active, not passive; suggests different techniques if some are not working well.
5. Assessment is not based on lengthy testing but on focused and pointed

interviewing, some assessment or testing, and observations (by the client as well as by the therapist).

6. Carrying out assignments, or "behavioral practice" is relied on where the client makes an effort to confront and overcome his/her difficulties; records of success/failure are kept; plans are revised; and so on until the early successes are matured and made more reliable for the client. Less and less reliance on the therapist is one result of this more focused approach.

It is not as if the behaviorists or other short-term therapy advocates thought of all these procedures first. Franz Alexander delineated some procedures remarkably similar about forty years ago when he said:[11]

> Like the adage, nothing succeeds like success, there is no more powerful therapeutic factor than the performance of activities which were formerly neurotically impaired or inhibited. *No insight, no emotional discharge, no recollection can be as reassuring* as accomplishment in the actual life situation in which the individual failed (Italics added).

And, same reference:

> Thus the ego regains that confidence which is the fundamental condition, the prerequisite, of mental health. Every success encourages new trials and decreases inferiority feelings, resentments, and their sequelae — fear, guilt, and resulting inhibitions.

Franz Alexander was a successful, devoted, and highly-regarded psychoanalyst at the Chicago Institute of Psychoanalysis when he wrote this passage. Why, then, did not more people realize the saliency of this viewpoint and take up with short-term psychotherapy more vigorously? It is hard to answer this query scientifically, as no research appears to have been done on this specific issue. Suffice it to say that the analysts had "other fish to fry" in the form of making more and more of their viewpoint, garnishing it here and there and, of course, keeping clients for longer time meant more money from less turnover of clients/patients, a matter not to be wholly neglected in trying to understand the forces supporting long-term psychotherapy, especially in the USA. World War II and the ensuing activation of community mental health clinics throughout the country gave a strong impetus to developing short-term therapy since more and more people were calling for some kind of mental health help.

Bloom[12] has also identified a list of propositions guiding the short-term therapy effort. Their similarity to some cited above is apparent (paraphrased): Identify focal problem or problems; respect client strengths, don't underestimate him/her; be prudently active and selective about what is reacted to; present interpretations (notions, ideas, etc.) hesitantly, and ask for client reactions; encourage expression of emotion by client; note that problem solving begins in the interview and is carried out in real life situations; keep to a time structure; don't try to cover too much ground or see each problem as different and distinct; avoid emphasis on factual questions; don't stress the precipitating event too much (this stricture may be considered somewhat moot by many short-term therapists, as the precipitating events often belong to a larger class of events and better understanding and control might lead more reliably to behavior change); avoid getting off on other topics; avoid overestimating the self-awareness (and, at first, self-control) of the client, allowing proper time for assimilating ideas leading to changed behavior.

One might add to these points that the bottom line is behavior change, no matter how much feeling change, perceptual change, etc. appear to occur. As the Alexander quote, above indicates, "No insight, no emotional discharge, no recollection can be as reassuring as accomplishment in the actual life situation . . ."

One practice that is followed by many short-term therapists is to give "homework assignments" to be engaged in outside the therapy hour.[13] This practice carries the work of the therapy session out into the client's real world and validates the changes there, as well as allowing a critical assessment of what takes place in therapy itself. It is important that therapy be seen as something other than a strictly confidential relationship to the therapist, important as that is; that it be seen as a wide ranging *modus operandi,* and as a kind of training for and training in instrumentation or implementation. After all, what brought the client to therapy was his/her distress in real life, as observed by the client or by important or significant others. Not to refer to these instigating or baseline conditions is folly, wasteful, disrespectful, and arrogant on the part of the therapist; a practice the client should not let the therapist get away with.

CRISIS INTERVENTION

One of the most important forms of brief or short-term psychotherapy is crisis intervention.[14] As the term implies, this notion describes the reactions of persons who meet a situation with which they cannot momentarily cope. These situations may arise, as we all know, from unexpected trauma in one's life — the death or serious injury of a loved one, an unexpected illness, a job loss, a severe financial reversal, and so on. Other crisis-provoking situations may include sudden and heretofore unexpected reactions to what are called "developmental crises," such as might occur with the birth of a child, marriage, divorce, or the like. While the latter have some history behind them, the immediate reaction to the event is often traumatizing to people and they react as if a crisis vastly different from their general living were at hand. Crises are usually situational to a considerable extent, although not exclusively so. The woman who has a postpartum crisis reaction is responding to a number of things — responsibility, concretely changed plans, etc. — she might well have anticipated long beforehand, but didn't, hence the crisis reaction is more than just the facts occasioned by the birth of a child. The same can be said for divorce, marriage, job loss, and so on as these are often open to clear anticipation to the wary, or to people who observe their environments, interpersonal and otherwise, with caution and equanimity.

However, the immediate and compelling aspect of crisis intervention is situational and calls for a quick-response type of therapy found in the literature on psychotherapy by a host of writers.[15] These include police work, rescue squads, fire fighters, as well as crises handled by psychologists, social workers, and psychiatrists in community mental health clinics, schools, and in private practice. The advent of "emergency" numbers in communities permitting a call-in service is an example of crisis intervention that may range all the way from suicide attempts to homicide. A stitch in time saves nine, may be the guiding principle involved in much crisis intervention.[16]

Crisis intervention consists of a series of techniques that represent a relatively quick and precise response to emergencies in people's lives. For example, a student may call into an emergency number and say s/he is about to jump out of a tenth story window as a result of being jilted by a lover. The call is, obviously, for help; a way of asking for help that might deter this catastrophe. Rather than admonishing or moralizing with the student, the careful crisis worker will try to elicit how the depressed one arrived at the present state in terms of recent events, how the person feels about the lost relationship, how angry the offended person is, and so on. The therapeutic response is a "cooling off" one, not advice or probing or censurship; all that would only risk making the disturbed person more anxious and resentful and thereby more likely to jump.

One patient called me at 3 a.m. one Sunday, saying, "I'm going to kill her, so help me God, I'm going to kill her," as the opening statement. This is a bit of a large message to get when one is awakened out of one's sleep. The client did not say who he was, nor give any other details, only that highly emotionally charged opening response. What did I do? I said, "Well, I can understand you are very upset with her (recognizing who he was by this time), can you tell me more about what just happened?" He replied with a barrage of invectives about his girlfriend, missing the point of my message to him. After he calmed down some I again asked him if he could tell me what precipitated his upset (referring to his call as an "upset" was not value-ridden, accusatory, or otherwise inhibitory), and he then began to say she had jilted him that evening earlier, and he had been trying to decide if he would, indeed, seek her out (with her new lover) and kill one or both of them. After about fifteen minutes of cliff-hanging talk, we closed off the phone conversation with the invitation for him to call me the next day about noon and let me know how he was feeling and what further notions he had about the problem and his upset. This he did, much more calmly, and we decided on a fuller interview the following day, Monday, in which the whole matter was reviewed. On this occasion I reminded him that I thought he could have seen this crisis brewing from what he had told me, and I wondered if he could prepare himself better for what might be her resolution to leave him. We worked out matters this way and in relation to some potential alternative he had, all of which allowed him to not only feel better but to gain some purposeful action and direction. This crisis, different from the anonymous student calling in, cited above, was a person whom the writer had known in therapy, but had not suspected as being so volatile. In the crisis intervention with the student, the immediate goal was to prevent suicide; and, following that, to offer him an appointment to discuss his situation, a matter that should take place as soon as possible; or even be followed, if possible, by someone going to his apartment — with his permission, of course — to immediately work out things better. The 3 a.m. call, coming from a client already in therapy, had more known possibilities, involving as it did in this instance, a kind of temporizing with the client, leading to more detailed help and support following soon.

While we can say each crisis situation is somewhat different, there are also similarities such as taking the person's emotional response immediately and fully into consideration, encouraging talking as an alternative to disastrous action, keeping the discussion going long enough to allow for some emotional relief, and following through with the more substantial opportunity for the person to have a more lengthy and detailed session with a therapist, or have time and opportunity to deal closely with a friend or relative who might be more available than a therapist.[17]

Another aspect of crisis intervention, especially with cases where unexpected events overtake one, such as with accidents, disasters, death, is that they occur for reasons unrelated to the suffering one. That is, if the spouse of a woman is killed in a hunting accident, the grief reaction is both a traumatic one and one not usually related to the personality or problem status of the one left behind. Grief reactions have predictable features, a sequelae, and a longer-term set of relationships between the suffering one and his/her environment over time, including interpersonal relationships with other sufferers and friends related to the crisis-ridden one. These kinds of crisis events are not related to any psychopathology in the sufferer, and need to be treated as soon as possible as natural crises calling for unusual adjustments, acceptance, and preparation for carrying on without the lost one.[18] The carrying-on feature after the trauma or loss consists in defining the tasks one has to perform in the absence of the lost one, e.g., caring for the children in the case of a member of a marriage who has lost a spouse; finding a new job when one has been unexpectedly dismissed from a position; and so on. Timely intervention in these ways does not erase the problem, but it may present the suffering one from slipping further into depression, or failure to cope. Intervention may also modify secondary injury to others, psychologically, such as children who suffer from the loss of a parent or sibling or from the parent's reaction to job loss or the like. This is a kind of "preventive intervention," designed to ameliorate, not eradicate or dissolve a crisis situation.[19]

It is important to realize that crisis does not occur in a social vacuum, nor are crises wholly novel. Everyone in his life experiences crises, some of a passing nature, some more momentarily disturbing, some with long-range consequences. All of these crises occur in a social setting that affects not only the victim, the one having the crisis, but standers-by, as well, and those intimately connected with the suffering one. Whatever others can do to support the victim of a crisis can go a long way in helping weather the emotional implications of the loss; and while others cannot take away the problem nor the grief, they can support, stand by, and help out in small ways the adjustment of the suffering one over time. The whole purpose of crisis intervention, most simply stated, is proper, timely, continuing support which, of course, has longer-range ameliorative and preventive consequences.

There are some crises, however, that appear to have a history. That is a person has knowingly engaged in risk taking or ill-advised behavior, knowing full well that some untoward events might overtake him or her. When the crisis comes, one might say, "S/he should have seen this coming . . . sooner or later I knew this would happen . . ." And so forth. Sometimes people take a dim view of a person not preparing him/herself for "the inevitable," but that kind of moralizing does not go very far in helping the sufferer, and certainly does not help the loved ones also affected by the crisis.[20] The same compassion, support, acceptance, new planning, and so on all need to occur in this "careless" variety of crisis intervention just as much as with the unexpected variety. However, in the more careless version — if we can call it that — the victim has to consider self-examination to the point of possibly serious preventive work. A young man of the writer's acquaintance flaunted danger in his motorcycle riding, racing, and risk taking (the latter on regularly travelled roads). He came to a serious impasse on a city street when he misjudged distance and speed and ended up in the hospital for several months, losing his job, his cycle, and other cherished possessions in the wake of the accident. All of these consequences caused him to undergo therapy in quest of a saner, more reliable way of living in order to protect and extend the accomplishment of other values in his life (such, e.g., as concern for his two small children, his wife, and the nature of his new job after the accident).

Crisis intervention has also arisen for what one might call, partly, "political" reasons. That is, during the late 1960s and early 1970s, youth were often described as part of a "counter culture," and among their other rejections of society and conventionality, rejected the usual avenues of help and support.[21] Call-in centers and other crisis intervention methods sometimes arose in connection with this "counter culture movement." Often as not, these people were drug or alcohol involved, or perhaps suffered from social/emotional problems that were the outgrowth of substance abuse problems. Perhaps the greatest spurt to publicly supported crisis intervention arose in this connection on university campuses as well as in communities at large. Sometimes these crises involved getting the victims into more stable and wholesome living circumstances, getting them "dried out," after over use of alcohol, getting them passage home to family and friends away from an alien and unsupportive environment, and so on. There appears to be no end, then, to the crisis type of response to human difficulties, covering problems precipitiously befalling one, out to more chronic and ill-advised ways of living.

IS CRISIS INTERVENTION EFFECTIVE?

There are no clear and certain ways to answer this query, although it is a legitimate question. We do not have control cases who experience no crises, and we have poor or no access to persons who experience crisis and fail to find a satisfactory crisis intervention support. However, it is possible to follow-up on what has happened to some crisis intervention cases to ascertain how they have been helped and what some of the outcomes are.

We can structure the reply to this query by pointing up some important features of a systematic nature that characterize crisis intervention. While this will not answer the research question adequately, it will provide some clarity. Ewing summarized the main features of crisis intervention as follows: Brevity and ready availability; self-limiting (usually last no longer than 5 to 6 weeks, except where people enter regular therapy); attrition is high (i.e., most people just want a momentary assuagement or support and do not see the need for longer-term help, even if the longer-term still means short-term psychotherapy); the intervention is intended to return the person to his/her precrisis level of functioning; sometimes new copying skills are indicated, however, that while crisis intervention is supportive and ameliorative, it may also need, in some cases, to be problem solving, hence sustained over some period of time beyond the immediate crisis; the therapist role is largely nontraditional, and calls on the therapist to react only to the present situation in an active and participatory way, not nondirectively nor passively; and, lastly, while crisis intervention is not, per se, therapy, it may well prepare the individual for the much needed therapy, especially if the crisis is of a discernibly larger piece of the person's life.

Given this context, then, it is easy to see that crisis intervention is difficult to research competently. However, some stabs have been made. One such research stance is that of assessing a potential treatment group in a clinic, giving crisis intervention help to a random group, then following these out for a period of weeks to be compared to those not related in a crisis way, but given more sustained therapy.[22] Some uncontrolled results are shown by Parad and Parad (1968) in which records of 98 clinics that offered crisis intervention were surveyed, involving 1,165 cases.[23] Although based on therapist records — it would be almost impossible to follow-up this many clients from so large an assortment of clinics — the judged outcome was that 68 percent were improved. Shaw et al. (1968) referred 227 child guidance clinic cases, covering a 12-month follow-up period, and found 56 percent of the crisis intervention cases (children) were either "improved" or "much improved," and 62 percent of the parents were likewise rated. Using pre-, post-, and follow-up questionnaires, Donovan et al.[24] (1981) followed up on 43 participants in an 8-week crisis intervention program (not the most commonly accepted definition of crisis intervention, it must be said), and reported that 91 to 95 percent of the clients found the group helpful or they liked the group. How much their behavior changed, we do not know. One valuable kind of data that we do not now have would follow these persons for (say) 2 to 5 years to see if they returned for any kind of crisis intervention and thereby compare them with regular admissions to mental health facilities for noncrisis induced help.

The latter point is approximated in a study by Langsley et al. (1968)[25] in which crisis intervention methods were compared to hospitalization. They randomly assigned 150 applicants for hospitalization to crisis intervention and compared their outcomes to 150 assigned to hospitalization. Results showed "on subjective measures" of personal functioning, family adjustment and social relationships that the crisis intervention cases were doing as well as the hospitalized patients after 6 and 18 months follow-up points; and that on more objective measures — number and duration of subsequent hospitalizations — the crisis patients scored lower on both measures. The economy involved in reducing costly hospitalization, aside from the personal matters involved for at least a wide array of people commonly seen in crisis situations.

In summary, crisis intervention studies tell us several things about short-term psychotherapy and about therapy in general. First, such work tells us that people may undergo profound crises and recover in due time and without profound and long-term help. Second, most crises arise from exigencies in peoples' lives for which they have poor or little preparation. Responding to the crisis may help them get their houses in order and thus be instructive of better living. A third outcome from crisis intervention is that it is a viable alternative to hospitalization and should likely be resorted to more often in place of hospitalization simply because it is both more economical and more beneficial to the client. Lastly, crisis intervention is one long arm of short-term psychotherapy and should be so viewed and promoted. Insofar as it is a response to critical need, it may also help prevent the crystallization of disturbance and thereby contribute to emotional help and health. Crisis help occurs without resort to long-term help which has often arisen from neglect of remediable problems in a timely way.

Chapter 2

WHY DO PEOPLE SEEK PSYCHOTHERAPY?

THE BASIC QUESTION is why people seek psychotherapy. Most people do not stop to ponder this question. They think, first, of seeking help from professionals rather than considering more fully how they can help themselves, or how they can utilize informal relationships with others to help themselves (and possibly others, too, in the same interaction).

Among people seeking help, the commonest diagnosis used is "depression." Depression appears to occur in the wake of almost any interruption in our lives, whether it is a medical or physical problem or a psychological or social problem. When you have a cold, the "flu," or even a painful toothache, one of the reactions is that of depression. The body slows down, interest lags, motivation is depleted, and most people just "want to be left alone" at such times. Depression is so common that one would feel something was unusual or wrong if no depressive aftermath was observed following any kind of medical (physical) or psychological problem. When people feel depressed, however, they think it is "abnormal" and they want immediate help to get over the feeling. They have not learned to ask questions about what has brought on the depression nor what the depressive reaction "means" in the larger sense of their lives. They just want to get over the depression, post haste. That is the point where they often turn to therapy for "the answers."

Popular articles appear often in newspapers and magazines about the "blues." We know, too, that the "blues" as a form of music (an American original!) gives expression to depressive reactions, to disappointments in life, and to the general vicissitudes of living. In dealing with the blues, people are admonished to "think positive," to "count their blessings," to "look to the brighter side of life," and so on. Thus, the common culture has, so to say, arisen to the call of the blues and attempted to give advice short of appealing to a therapist, taking drugs, consuming alcohol, going on a spending spree, and so forth. The common culture has said that the "blues" are natural and would seldom recommend formal steps to get rid of them. Take-them-in-stride, common sense advice says.

But the American culture (somewhat true of other cultures, but not as much so as in America) has said that a complaint deserves serious consideration: See your physician! See your dentist! See your psychologist! And so on. Turn over your problems to the expert and "get to the bottom" of the issues involved.[1] The symptom of depression "goes deeper," as some would say and bespeaks of more serious problems lurking behind the scenes, in the "unconscious," in one's past, issues that have been neglected, denied, repressed, and so forth and that are now arising out of neglect in the past. This more formidable view of personal difficulties — we are referring primarily here to depression, but the same responses would be found to almost any other psychological complaint — has been assumed by the common culture more typically in the past few decades, arising, in part, from the heritage of the Freudian culture, but also from the "quick fix," "fast foods" culture of present-day America. The latter seems contradictory to the former but isn't. The first emphasis — the Freudian one — sensitizes the latter "quick fixes." Both are unrealistic.

So we have, in effect, three sets of broadly-based cultural attitudes impinging on people: Take your blues in stride, that's life, keep your chin up, get on with daily living, keep on the stick, and so forth; against the more modern view that any problem is worth long-term serious consideration and may, in fact, be a serious, buried, and formidable affair. The ultra-modern view is get-it-done-by-quick fix.

How shall we differentiate between these sets of influence? How can therapy, even brief therapy of a few visits, encounter or confront these very different ways of looking at psychological problems and arrive at a sensible, economical, and useful set of answers? That is, of course, what much of this book is about, and we shall tackle part of this question right now, right here. Some ways for you as an individual client to proceed, and some ways for therapists to respond follow.

A TRIAL VISIT

One might make a trial visit to a psychologist, psychiatrist, social worker, or to a mental health clinic, a counseling center, or the like. One can consult the yellow pages of most city phone books for listings. One can also get names from friends who have consulted mental health clinicians (probably the best way), or one can call professional referral societies (all the professions have such referral services which, also, are often listed in the yellow pages of the phone book), or one can ask for referrals from one's physician, minister, teacher, guidance counselor at school, and so forth. There are plenty of sources of referral!

Upon making such an appointment, one can ask a series of questions about oneself, one's concerns, and so forth, and see if the mere asking and discussion brings relief, new thoughts, some restructuring of the problem (such as to make it seem, or be, less formidable), receive some possible advice, and so forth. We know from a good deal of research that one-visit-only can be very helpful; in fact, the modal number of visits to private practitioners, to mental health clinics, to college and university counseling centers is *one visit.* (We'll come back to that issue later for more examination of what it means.)[2]

It is best to have prepared, then, a list of descriptions of what ails one, what the nature of the complaints are (when they occur), something of their intensity, how long they last, what one does to cope with them, and so forth. The better prepared you are, the better any therapist can help you — don't rely exclusively or completely on the therapist, no matter how uncomfortable you feel you are, how good the therapist is reputed to be, or how seriously the problem is considered. You are there seeking help because you feel you need HELP. You are not crying "help" like a drowning person — although you may feel that way at times — but you are seeking some kind of outside advice, perspective, support, a deliberate move, not a crisis reaction.

In fact, this one visit may be just what you need to get back on your own, find the best direction, cope better, feel happier, and so forth. We hope so.

In making this first visit, come prepared, as has been suggested. Tell your story in factual terms, staying away from presumed diagnosis, or trying to "explain" your feelings and behavior. Just tell it like it is. Two contrasting types of first interview "stories" are shown below to suggest how you might proceed.

> Mabel was talking about her problems to her therapist (or the person she expected to be her therapist), a woman. She said she was 'through with men,' and had no hopes of being successful with men on a serious basis. Men were just no-damned-good in her book. She spoke of her short-term affairs to the therapist, saying they all ended (without specifying how long some of them had lasted) on 'sour notes,' owing to the ill will of the men involved. Her problems were those arising from being victimized by others. What was her explanation?[3] She had been "stood up," lied to, promised trips or gifts, or the like, only to find she had been "given a lot of blarney." She had tried very hard to be fair to the men involved, to hold her own in the relationship, to expect and give on an equal footing, but somehow she had always been disappointed, taken advantage of, even deceived by the men. The whole story was about how awful men were! The therapist in this case was wise enough to know what had been going on in Mabel's rendition of her distress: She had not said anything about what *she* had done, or not done, how she coped with this succession of men, how she felt she might be helped by therapy to develop better and longer lasting relationships and so on. She was just there to damn men as completely as she could, and to have the therapist agree she had been deceived — and weren't those horrible men despicable.
>
> The therapist was wise enough and experienced enough to say, in effect, "Now what do you think I can do about these terrible men you are telling me

about?" "Or, possibly, is there something we can talk about in *life* in more specific ways that seems to allow you, even encourage you, to get involved with hopeless relationships with men, such as to give you your present plight?" The woman was somewhat shocked at these questions at first, then after some thinking, she said, "You mean *I* can do something about these men and how they affect me?" The therapist, of course, said "yes," and then they began to discuss some ways in which she could begin to intervene in her own behalf.

To make a longer story short — she was seen for 6 visits — she began to concern herself with three general problem areas: How she first met men, what she and they said, how attracted she was, how she responded to first overtures, and so on. It turned out that she was so eager for a relationship, she gave in on all counts to the men — went home with them and went to bed with them the first evening, or immediately following their meeting, called them the next day to propose a date for lunch or dinner or a movie; called them again a day or two later if the first call did not produce her hoped-for good results, and generally plagued them with her "need to see them again soon . . ."

A second type of relationship she pursued with men was to begin to talk seriously to them about marriage by about the third date (if she got that far!), often not directly but certainly indirectly, giving the men, presumably, that she was eager for a fast, closed-off, serious relationship with marriage the certain objective. She overwhelmed most men, it would appear.

A third way of relating to them had to do with her petulance and anger if matters did not turn out to her liking — if they did not accept the need for a second date right away, or appreciate her overtures, and the like. "I've-given-so-much, you-so-little — what's-wrong?" attitude. This intended interest turned sour as she overwhelmed the men she felt she was interested in or those she felt should be interested in her ("after all, we had *so* many things in common").

The therapist at first listened to a kind of "verbal scenario," based on what Mabel had said in her first visit. This scenario did not say much about what went on *between* herself and her men — how, for example, they replied to her insistent overtures and how she replied, how the conversations progressed, in some detail, but only her lamentations at not being as well-received as she felt she needed to be. The therapist pointed out how much this scenario left out of the relationship, how victimized she appeared to be, and how easily and quickly she was discouraged, turned-off, and then turned to the next man whom she felt some attraction to and whom she calculated would be the "answer to my prayers." Mabel began to see how one-sided, selfish, self-serving and headed-for-disaster her relationships with men were. She began to see herself as "wheelhorse cut loose and beginning to run amok," a probably pretty good description.

During Mabel's second visit to her therapist, they discussed one current relationship Mabel was sharing with a man, one she had met only the previous weekend at a dance. They looked at how Mabel's approach worked, what she said and did, how she felt about the early success of her overtures, how the man reacted, how he probably felt, and they went into some fine-grained details about the interactions. Mabel began to see how forward, presumptive, and demanding she was, especially at the beginning of a relationship. She soon began to pull back some, talk and presume less, and try to listen to and observe what the man was saying and doing. She had already by the time of the second therapy visit, encountered the current gentleman of her desire the second time ("second date the very next evening — I was really going strong," she said), and upon uttering that statement, took a deep breath and said, "there I go again, pushing him to something I want" and then she began to cry and say, "What makes me act that way?" She had begun in the second visit to the therapist to doubt some of her interpersonal tactics and to open up consideration of other motives, other ways of relating to men, and to setting aside her inordinate desire to have her way fully with the man. This questioning of herself began to lead to somewhat different approaches to men and also to different approaches to people in her office. As is often the case, one's particular problem area — say, as in Mabel's case, with men — bespeaks of other relationships where one may encounter similar problems. It turned out that Mabel had had three female roommates in the past 15 months, owing to the fact — as she quoted them saying — "They could not agree with me on how to run the house, get groceries, pay the bills, share the phone, and so forth," which, upon more discussion turned out to be very reminiscent of how she dealt with men. The female relationships with roommates, then, came into the discussion about men and the concept of her "pushiness" became increasingly more evident. What helped her to relent on her insistence that others do her bidding was that such tactics almost always failed. Even if they appeared to succeed for a time, the longer-range likelihood was that they would turn sour and, after a time, lead her to the negative reactions she so frequently encountered with men who "played along for a while" with her. Mabel began to see that she had a "style of interrelating," as she put it, that was excessively demanding and selfish and that she would be better off if she slowed down some, took her time, considered the other person more fully (whether the other person was a man, a roommate, an office mate, or someone else with whom she had some potentially continuous relationship).

There is a lot more to Mabel's therapeutic story, as one might expect. We cannot cover everything. Suffice it to say that Mabel progressed well. She went on vacation for three weeks after her third therapy session, taking along ideas of how to relate more appropriately (and, it was hoped, more successfully) with men, some of which she tried out during the vacation period. She reported at her fourth therapy hour that she had met two men while on vacation, did not pursue either one of them in her usually vigorous and demanding manner, and found one of them clearly not to her liking (although at first, she admitted, she felt "he was gorgeous!" but upon closer scrutiny felt he was not very interesting in the larger sense) and so let the prospect of dating him drop even though he proposed the second date. The other seemed to appeal to her more, but she was waiting to hear from him when he came into her city on business to judge if there was some possibility of a more enduring and satisfying relationship between them. She noted, however, that this man lived over 500 miles away and there was little value in trying to make something of the relationship on the hopes that either one would, romantically, rush to the other's city and live happily ever after. Realism had begun to appear!

Mabel had two more visits. She felt she had learned what she wanted to know; had changed, in principle, what needed changing. She now sought the life experiences that would enable her to build on them for marriage or for some long-range result. She began to meet men, enjoy their company on an "as is" basis (as she put it), without strings attached, and she began to feel she was understanding both men and herself more fully. A follow-up a year later revealed that she had recently become engaged to be married and had bought a house with her fiancee; she said he had "pursued her . . . not vigorously, not insistently, but encouragingly and consistently . . ." and that she had matured into a really good relationship after all these debacles over the past 10 years.

WHAT WAS MABEL'S PROBLEM?

Why did Mabel seek psychotherapy? She was unhappy. She was beginning to be very negative about men and thus perhaps about to cut herself off from real relationship possibilities. She was depressed. In filling out a diagnostic form, Mabel was diagnosed as "depressed," and a number given her reaction in order to get insurance support for her therapy costs. But the diagnosis was only a semantic thing. Her problem was that she was selfish, selfish to a degree that spoiled her most important relationships and certainly most other ones much of the time. What we call her, in the diagnostic sense, is not important; what we do *for* and *with* her is much more important. The language used by her and by the therapist centered around her being impulsive, jumping-the-gun, insistent on her way, and so on; these were the terms that fit her life, that showed how she acted and felt, that explained why others behaved toward her as they did; these were the meaningful notions that had to be hammered out into new shapes in her everyday life. These are the behavioral and "diagnostic" concepts the average person can react to and understand; we do not need a lot of highfaluting language to describe Mabel and her efforts to live more happily, relate better, and understand and control her own behavior more successfully. While Mabel might have needed professional help — especially at this time and in terms of her readiness to seek and use help, although very hesitantly at first —

she also needed to begin to work out things for herself under some minimal, but effective, ways with a therapist. Given a bit of judicial help, she could begin to go-it-on-her-own, and she did. A few months or a few years earlier, Mabel might have refused help and not been able to use it effectively even though help might have been available. She got "ready" after a (to her) sufficient length of time after observing that what she wanted was unduly frustrating and unlikely to produce good results. It took time for her to get ready for therapy, more time than the therapy itself!

Also, it is important to point up that Mabel's "diagnosis" changed. Whereas she was diagnosed "depressed" for reimbursement purposes, and she was "mistreated by men" from her vantage point, she really was selfish, unilateral, impulsive, etc. from a more objective, descriptive standpoint. Her depression "lifted" (think, now, how that term is used, suggesting a cloud over one that lifts and lightens, something outside, away from, unrelated to, oneself — a very misleading notion) and she became more optimistic, more realistic, and actually did develop new and different and more satisfying relationships. Although one might think the story of Mabel had a "fairytale" ending — she did become engaged and married — the "living happily every after" part we do not yet know about — it also had a realistic ending, one that she had sought as a normal matter (it *was* normal for her to have an abiding, satisfying relationship with a man — her objectives were reasonable, her methods not). But help was needed in bringing about these ends.

Why didn't we think that Mabel's relationship with a man was an offshoot of her relationship with her father, or with some aspects of her mother-father relationships; where, possibly, her father was the intractible person her mother always curried favor with, sought to please, and suffered quietly and desperately at not achieving these goals. Well, her parents were not, knowingly, that estranged or onesided in their relationship. There were no easy explanations of her problems from her past, no "models" she lived by unconsciously and tried to resolve, vicariously in her present, ever doomed because she had not solved the "first problem" in her life which came about at the hands of her parents. This latter view would have sent her into long-term, intensive psychotherapy and taken perhaps years at the rate of several times a week, costing into the tens-of-thousands of dollars, and still not netted — insofar as we know from research on psychoanalysis or psychodynamic psychotherapy — her the results she wanted, or perhaps, netted them so grudgingly and late that they would have served less than satisfactory purposes. The short-term context of stressing the here-and-now, stressing how she actually behaved vis-a-vis important others, and how she evaluated these matters, all going on daily in her life, was the productive way to proceed. The 6-session format provided a lot for Mabel; it might not work for all people, yet it might work for most, and for some even in a shorter time. Remember, the modal (most frequent) number of interviews in clinics and even in private practice is *one* visit, and the mean (average) in mental health settings is between four and eight visits; Mabel was right in the middle of this range: 6 visits.

ALEX, A SHORT-TERM CASE

Alex was a very likeable, outgoing, fair-haired, grinning 21-year-old lad who was about to graduate college. He had much anxiety upon presentation of himself for therapy, owing, he said, to his not knowing what he was going to do upon leaving school. He had just a few months to get ready — by June — having presented himself for therapy about the first of March, same year.

Alex presented himself in the following manner:

> I just feel I am lost. I don't know what to do upon graduation. My major is music, but I am not good enough to make my living at it in an orchestra or band (I play the reed instruments — you know what they are?) (the therapist nodded "yes"). I have a minor in what is called here "Business Methods" which is a mixture of accounting, selling, economics, statistics, and marketing, and I have learned some new things and see some new prospects for me in this area, but I have only taken these courses in the last year or so, and I am unsure of them having much relevance for me. I may sound like a "vocational case," which my roommate calls me, but I lie awake nights, I have trouble concentrating. I have argued more with my girlfriend whom I have liked very much — and we *may* be serious about each other in the long run if I don't louse it up with my moodiness — and I have argued over the phone with my parents who want me to continue with music since I said I wanted that and I do have a major in it. I just don't know what to do and the problems are causing me headaches, sleeplessness, grouchiness, intolerance of others, and . . . well . . . lots of things I don't like.

Diagnostically we might consider Alex anxious, depressed, or even hysterical, if the latter seemed to propel him into a lot of impulsive, ill-considered, self-defeating behaviors, but, overall, he was more anxious than anything else. He had depressive features, too, but not as pronounced as the anxiety. We gave him an "Anxiety Neurosis" diagnosis so we could proceed with his insurance reimbursement. We could not "treat" anxiety; we could only treat his behavior and feelings in their daily context.

Alex shaped up so fast we could not believe it. He said after one session that he was not good enough for competitive musicianship — he knew and admitted that — but he could play-for-kicks, as he put it, in dance bands, in the local church orchestra, and now and then for weddings and other such occasions. He had taken a bit of a whirl at arranging for dance bands in the first three years of his college career (abandoned the senior year because he was taking extra courses in the business curriculum). Although taking some other courses that might help him vocationally, he saw clearly by his last semester that, there, too, he did not have enough skill to compete well in the business world. He was not interested in graduate work such as would be available in an MBA degree (Masters in Business Administration, a popular degree of late).

Alex's principle conflict was between his announced major — music, and what it would offer him in life — on the one hand, and his growing realization that he could not compete effectively in this area. Mabel's conflict was between her desires for a man and her methods (and results associated therewith) versus her feedback indicating that all was not well with her in this (and, later, in other) departments of her life. Alex, however, came to his realizations sooner, perhaps the issues were less formidable, less serious, less difficult to change, less long-lived in his behavioral economy, compared to Mabel. Perhaps so. But perhaps, also, Alex was more ready to change and so an opportunity for change was mobilized more readily and effectively.

Alex later said, "Well I can work in a music store, be around music, sell instruments, demonstrate them, give lessons to kids on the side, play some in bands and orchestras on a not too competitive basis, and get along for a while. I can decide later if I want to run a music business or go into some other kind of business, and meanwhile use music entirely as a hobby." He had begun to put together these options upon one encounter with a therapist, arriving at this formulation in the first hour as the therapist helped him put together the fact that he was trying to please his parents. Both parents were part-time musicians, and the whole family had been "a musical family" with two siblings being rather accomplished instrumentalists and already securely employed in orchestras. The conflict in career choice was made more real for him when his parents learned he had chosen the business courses the last year, especially the last semester of his college career, and objected strenuously. They felt he should have been learning some previously untried reed instruments such as the oboe and the bassoon (he had formerly pursued almost exclusively the clarinet and the saxophone, with some interest in the flute). Having enrolled in the business courses — two the fall semester, three the spring semester just before graduation — showed him he did have some interest in this area. Although he doubted he could pursue it wholly as an alternative to music, this budding interest was to be acknowledged, dealt with and, moreover, dealt with in the light of his parents' attitudes. How would he do that? Would they understand? Would they feel he was a "dropout from the family" (his words) because he was not pursuing a musical career as had all the rest of the family? And so on. No wonder he could hardly sleep! No wonder he was irritable and short-fused emotionally with his girlfriend and others.

There are always reasons for people consulting a therapist at a given time (other than being coerced by others or given some kind of official ultimatum: get help or get out of school, leave the job, or go to jail). For Alex it was the coming to the end of the year and his impending graduation, together with the implications he would go straightforwardly into a musical career which meant, by implication, the same kinds his family had pursued, as nothing else would be acceptable.

Alex had two therapy interviews, the one described in some detail above, and a second one two weeks later. He indicated at the end of the first interview that he saw the possibilities of putting together a "secondary, compromise career," as he phrased it, made up of working in a music store, doing a lot of musically-related activities, teaching music some on the side to children, and learning the music business as he would any other business. He had a job opportunity in a city near his parental home, but far enough away to promote some independence from his family. He also averred in the first interview that some of the subject matter in his business courses intrigued him somewhat, especially the marketing and selling and, since he knew music well and instruments very well, he could take a confident stance toward the buying public and enjoy it, all the while learning the business from a more technical standpoint.

But this was an easy problem, you say, not nearly as complicated or long-lasting as was Mabel's problem. Perhaps. Alex mentioned in his second interview that he had about decided he would follow the joint music business and music-on-the-side opportunity he had. He had told this to his family during the weekend following his first therapy visit. His parents were somewhat taken aback, he reported, but over the weekend several discussions were held and there was some agreement/adjustment on their part and on his part. At least, he averred, he was not "leaving music behind completely," and he could still learn the business to advantage while pursuing *some* music (the emphasis on the "some" personified his family's feelings about compromising with him, saying he was not thoroughly rejecting music). The family also agreed he was not expected to be as much of a classical musician as his siblings (they were both employed in symphonic and concert musical organizations, whereas he had pursued from the start more popular music and was not as much of a technical expert as the siblings were, and everyone had long known this).

In the light of our discussion about therapy, diagnosis, short-term emphasis, and getting help with important decisions and actions forthwith, what can be said about Alex's apparently quick recourse to a workable decision? A follow-up a year later revealed he was working in the music store, doing the other things he had planned on, was agreeably satisfied with these decisions/actions, and had become engaged to his college girlfriend. He had lost his worrisome complaints and symptoms.

He revealed in the second therapy meeting that he had the previous summer, upon experiencing some headaches and lots of worrying, consulted a therapist (psychoanalyst), upon the advice of the family physician. The analyst took the viewpoint we might expect by holding that Alex's complaints were due to felt rejection and invidious comparisons to his siblings by his parents and that he was suffering from these strong feelings of rejection, neglect, and the like. He was with the analyst for about three months (during the summer between his junior and senior year of college) but judged, in retrospect, the experience — he had about 35 sessions at the rate of three times a week for about three months — as not very helpful and as missing the point of his concerns. We cannot dismiss the fact that he had this much therapy which might have started up some self-reflection that was useful, but no points of departure were identified and no movements toward a solution were activated. When he obtained the very short-term therapy at the university counseling center he was "ready" to work more fully on his problem and, given some direction in a conceptual sense and some implications he had already thought of as directions he could take, he responded well and moved ahead toward a solution. He also had derived some more confidence in the realization that his problem of career choice and the resulting symptomatology related to conflicts about values, precedences, family expectations, etc. were fairly normal reactions. He saw that many young people had such problems, that there were provisional ways to solve the issues and that the conflicts didn't mean he was a terrible person about to let down his family and besmirch the musical tradition they held to so reverently.

And his problems did not mean he was suffering from the effects of some serious inferiority complex at the hands of his rejecting parents who, it was alleged, did not accept his less-than-great musical ability. True, he was not as gifted as his siblings — perhaps not as much as his parents — but these attitudes never kept him from pursuing music, and he had fitted into the family musical matrix pretty well all along, he felt. The issues of decisions and actions arose as he approached the end of his college work because graduation was to be followed by serious and intensive career pursuits. He had begun to lay the groundwork for his career in a kind of oblique way, admittedly, by taking the business courses, but that turned out not to be an aberration or a compensation, or a reaction-formation, or any other symptom-defense related matter; it turned out to be something he could plan for, act on, and use on a potential career basis. It worked out well, in short. And his solution to the problem of his career began to fit well into his family context; the family accepted and wished him well in his career. He did not feel they were grudging about it, nor that they reasserted he was simply compensating for his less-than-adequate musical talent and becoming a second class (family) citizen as a result.

TRIAL VISITS AND SHORT-TERM EFFORTS PAY OFF

Although somewhat different in several important respects, the trial visits (the first one is really a trial visit, even to a surgeon, a psychoanalyst, or whatnot) of both Mabel and Alex paid off. Mabel's problem took a bit more time and were in a sense somewhat more involved than Alex's problems. Yet Mabel rose to the therapeutic occasion and things worked out well for her, insofar as we can tell. Life is always changing and peoples' therapy, while it may assist a great deal at a given time and under given, limited circumstances, is no inoculation for life against adversity, pain, discouragement, or failure. Alex moved a bit faster, probably because the apparent combination of factors affording a solution were more available for him, plus the fact that his excursion into the psychoanalytic therapy may have readied him more for solutions than he or the second therapist thought to be the case. Both Alex and his analyst at first thought that his problems were "deep-seated" and "might take years to remedy," according to Alex's understanding and report on his psychoanalytic experience. However, many university and college counseling centers have scores of youth looking to interpersonal help, career decisions (decisions that imply or involve many emotional, social, and intense relationships) that have to be part of the complexity involved in arriving at career decisions. If all of them had to go into intense, long-term psychotherapy, how would counseling centers and community mental health centers ever function constructively and productively? Human behavior is complicated, to be sure, but not in the ways envisaged by the long-term, psychodynamically-oriented therapist; that route is not recommended for anyone but those who desire it, after thoughtful and investigative decision-making (even though that decision can be challenged by parallel cases of equal disturbance who arrive at more modest but equally good — or better — solutions to their problems).

Did Alex's problems or focus change in therapy? Yes and no. Some change in that the horrors of disappointing his family were modified and allowed to open up alternative routes. If we had held to the psychodynamic diagnosis of his problem, we would have to say his diagnosis changed considerably. But if we held to the notions extant in mental health clinics, in short-term therapy, in career help that is cognizant of extenuating emotional and social and familial conditions, we would have to say his problem attack and solution were altogether economical, realistic, and straightforward. His problems were what they seemed to be, even admitting a few side issues. Since the presenting problem — what was felt, noticed, perplexing, etc. to the individual — was where we started and, for the most part, that was where the matter stopped. Alex's problems, his plans and his future came to a provisionally successful conclusion albeit conclusions are ever final for now and all time — life is too complicated for that kind of outcome.

GENERAL REASONS FOR SEEKING THERAPY

The two illustrative cases of Mabel and Alex come close to home in delineating reasons why people consult therapists. However, they are not the whole set of reasons. A study was done of 100 consecutive male and 100 consecutive female applicants to a university counseling center; they were all seeking psychotherapy.[4] These students, ages 17 to 33, with the mean about 23 to 24 years, answered the Mooney Problem Checklist, which is a 300 item compilation of problems people experience and/or suffer from. The problem areas are divided into 11 categories: health and physical development; finances and related; social and recreational; social-psychological, personal-psychological; courtship and related sex and marriage; home and family; morals and religion; adjustment to college; future vocational/educational plans; and curriculum and teaching procedures. Of these 11 categories, the highest scoring ones were those related to social and recreational activities, social-psychological, and personal-psychological. Future plans regarding educational/vocational plans and goals, as might be expected among college/university students, came close behind. People, then, are most concerned about their personal, social, and psychological experiences. The problems presented by Mabel and Alex fit clearly into these categories with Alex's falling, also, into the educational/vocational sphere.

Other studies have been done on what are loosely "presenting complaints," those matters naively stated, personally felt, intellectually understood (to a degree) to be the places "where it hurts" that bring people for psychological help. Sometimes people "hurt" in a variety of ways and will pick one or another of them – e.g., "I have headaches" – rather than admitting at the outset they have trouble controlling their anger because there is more apparent social approval for having headaches (it is sort of like a stomachache or a toothache, seemingly less personal and less incriminating) than in admitting some self-control or self-evaluation items.

Among the three broad categories cited above from the Mooney Problem Checklist, the most common items were those relating to moodiness or, as cited earlier on in this chapter, feeling "blue." "Feeling easily hurt," "feeling tired . . .," excessive daydreaming, and wondering about one's future success in life numbered among other frequently reported items on this Checklist among the 200 students studied. The more psychological items relating to depression, feeling too easily hurt and lacking "spunk," were more often reported by women; men, on the other hand, reported more often a failure to get exercise, and wondering about feeling lonely in relation to love and affection. Although sex differences exist in these matters, they are not outstanding differences, and both men and women share more common areas of concern than they do different ones.

It is highly likely, then, that anyone presenting him/her self for psychotherapy will have some complaints – possibly even the largest and most severe ones – in the areas of interpersonal relationship, self-esteem, moodiness, and feeling depressed. In turn, these areas of concern suggest *conflicts* in their lives, conflicts between what they want (or think they should have, pleasing themselves or some others inordinately much or inflexibly) versus what they are actually getting. In short, conflict is between what one wants and what one gets, just that simply; but often complicated by persons, circumstances, histories, and qualifications placed on the "wanting" and "getting" by the complaining person. In turn, again, these conflicts are not exactly simple — although they may be simply stated for purposes of easier communication — but lead to many ramifications.[5] For example, a person doubtful about his or her career objectives may feel s/he should not study hard or do well since it is not for sure those grades will mean anything significant for a possibly changed career (changing from music to business, per Alex, above); so why put forth that extra effort if it won't lead anywhere, the person asserts. Following this skepticism, ramifications into poor study skills, poor overall achievement, low self-esteem, social isolation may follow. We don't just have one easy problem, we have clusters of problems, and what we do about one or more of them — even the easiest and most accessible of the problems — may ramify widely into other areas. Having a personal/psychological/social problem is not like breaking your shoelace, a matter easily repaired. Rather, it is a bit more like having a persistently leaky basement that not only is an annoyance in its own right but may bring on health problems, mildew, decay of furniture and rugs, and may place a large burden on the general usefulness of the house. Problems ramify!

SERIOUS PROBLEMS NOT REQUIRED FOR THERAPY

One does not have to have a serious problem to qualify, so to say, for therapy. Any problem will do, if one feels that help is indicated. Of course, some people feel, as we have noted above, that the slightest problem means that they have to go to a specialist, whether the complaint is medical or psychological; and can quote instances in which people temporized all too long with serious problems, thinking they were only passing matters, only to find they were later in great trouble healthwise. On the other hand, some folks rush for help before they try to do something for themselves, given the problem time to be overcome, discuss it informally with others, or observe themselves better in order to see if the felt problem is related to some fairly obvious problem they can correct (e.g., feeling tired or depressed in relation to eating too little and to not getting enough protein, not concentrating well on important matters owing to allowing too many distractions to interfere and so on).

Since serious problems are not required to justify therapy (if one needs that!), small matters may be taken in for consultation and remedies and relief found forthcoming. We know from the Mooney Problem Checklist data cited above that a commonly felt range of problems exists, and that it is "perfectly normal" to have such complaints. Some may require more. Knowing that self-healing, self-control, and self-management are important ingredients in all manner of health matters — psychological or medical — is important to understand. These self-help matters have to take over for the best results to be obtained.

Chapter 3

THE MAIN THEORIES OF PSYCHOTHERAPY: I. PSYCHODYNAMIC AND BEHAVIORAL

THERE WOULD ALWAYS BE some dispute if one asked leading therapists which were the "main theories." The term "main" implies goodness, better results, better known, and so forth; all of which are worthy of some consideration. However, the main theories of therapies here are grouped together in terms of general outlook, theory, underlying assumptions, and the like. It is best to be parsimonious and modest in ascribing "mainness" to therapies; too many details leave one confused and do not tell the reader what to expect. We shall describe the main outlooks regarding psychotherapy as the following: Psychoanalytic/psychodynamic; behavioral; cognitive or cognitive/behavioral. Some would include those with a heavy biological/organic bias. We will, of course, be less interested in the last-named inasmuch as ascribing psychological problems to mainly organic or hereditary factors — while this may be true in some cases — does not well equip the average therapy-goer to enlightened seeking of help or knowing what to expect when therapy is sought.

PSYCHOANALYTIC/PSYCHODYNAMIC THERAPIES

Psychoanalysis as everyone knows began with Freud. His followers amended his theories and practices somewhat, but most of them adhered fairly closely to Freud. All of them variously stressed the importance of the unconscious, the importance of infantile experiences, the utilization of "defenses" to keep the person from having to admit weaknesses or unacceptable characteristics to oneself and/or to others, and the likely condition that therapy had to be intense and very long. The last part, the length of therapy seems to have grown longer and longer in the American culture than in Europe. While Freud saw patients for 5 or so times a week, he did not see them for the years so common in America. Some references to length of therapy indicate that pure psychoanalysis, or orthodox therapy of this kind, leads into the hundreds of hours, even a thousand or more hours. Psychodynamic or Freudian-like (modified) could take into the hundreds of hours, possibly three to five hundred.[1] The length of therapy is often assumed to be a measure of thoroughness and of amount of change, but there are no really hard data to support that assumption. In fact most studies conducted relating the length of therapy, even including short-term or brief psychotherapy, fail to show any consistent relationship between length and satisfactory outcome.[2] Among some proponents of long-term psychoanalytic therapy, results have shown that a number of clients/patients received their most noticed help early on in the therapy, within the first few months.[3] There are no substantial or validated reasons for considering long-term psychotherapy superior. One should know this and ponder it before applying for long-term psychotherapy under the assumption that something better or more long lasting will result. Many people enter therapy — both long-term and short-term — more than once and, given the time and money and incentive, therapy is as good as the two people performing it: the therapist and the client, but under the auspices of the theory.

The main assumption in long-term, psychoanalytic therapy is that the person's difficulties spring from deeply repressed childhood experiences too anxiety-provoking to admit into full consciousness. If one starts off with that assumption, then s/he is "sold a bill of goods," so to speak, at the outset. If that were true, no one would ever profit from short-term therapeutic efforts; it would be like trying to build a paper shack and call it a palace for luxurious living. Moreover, the "depth" of the person's makeup as the forbidden recesses in which the problems lie assumes further that one cannot change on his/her own; the analysis is necessary. Although psychoanalysis, like all therapies, seeks to give the client more control and understanding over his/her life, the avenue to this achievement is extremely rough and long-lasting via the "depth" route. This required length is matched by another assumption, viz., that the person does not know what is the driving force in the array of problems; they are "unconscious" according to psychoanalysis. However, one need only talk to a distressed person, or examine the rough spots in one's own life to know that there are daily many things done or not done that contribute to our distress. These are matters we need to put into better perspective, ones that lead to better self-control. This is true of sleeping and eating habits, exercise, dealing with significant others, handling routine matters in one's life, and so on. We change many of these rough spots without hardly noticing it, much of the time. Human behavior is exceedingly plastic while, at the same time, very stable; a compromise between these two is going on all of the time with us. Therapy that is efficient takes these crescendoes and decrescendoes for granted and attempts to remediate them to some practical extent, an extent useful for the person involved.

The social framework of treatment is also important in trying to understand psychotherapy values, choices, and results.

Data have shown for decades that the largest number of mentally ill, so-called, are from the lower classes, accounting for about twice as many seriously disturbed persons as their proportion in the total population.[4] How come the percentage of disturbed persons is so overwhelmingly related to social class (and economic condition as well)? Does the "mind" suppress these folks more than those more fortunately placed socially and economically? It seems highly unlikely. Rather, the explanation seems to lie more in the direction of personal and social resources for handling the vicissitudes of life. The better educated and higher socioeconomic groups do a better job of problem solving, although the latter people are the ones patronizing the psychoanalyst. By reason, however, and by concern for the mental health of the populace, the "sicker" persons (the lower class individuals, statistically speaking) should be the ones getting the more profound treatment. Rarely, if ever, does one find a lower class person in psychoanalysis (some may encounter "psychodynamically oriented" therapists in community mental health clinics, however, but these treatments are generally short-term, even very short-term with a national mean number of visits of 4, 5 or '6!).[5]

Psychoanalysis gets some of its supposed credence from the popular press. One is often amused by cartoons in *THE NEW YORKER* magazine that depict humorous interactions between analyst and patient (the patient is usually on the couch); the whole cartoon, while humorous and even poking fun at times at both patient and therapist, nonetheless sets this style or type of therapy up as common; psychoanalysis is presented as a synonym for therapy. It is interesting to note that other cartoons than those in *THE NEW YORKER* magazine often are more derisive of therapy or of psychoanalysis, often showing the patient/client as a kind of "Peck's bad boy," a misbehaving person who should be brought in line, and the like.

Since most patients in psychotherapy have been to more than one therapist, there is often a kind of "therapy referral network" operating informally. In studies at my university, we have found that 30 to 40 percent of the students we see in therapy have had previous therapy experience. People tend to refer each other to therapy, and when a patient becomes disenchanted with his/her therapist, or one or the other has to move, that person seeks the advice of friends known to have had, or currently being in, therapy. One writer even said that ". . . the major role of psychiatric clinics is to take in other professionals' wash . . ." This quote is not meant to demean psychotherapy, honest and valid attempts by therapist and patient to help the latter, but it does point up the social structure of help-seeking behavior, and to some aspects of therapy that may not be strictly therapeutic.

The male therapist-female patient syndrome also comes into the picture. There is very little evidence that gender couplings (male-male, female-female or cross sex couplings) are particularly potent one way or another where the matching is presumably open to scheduling time of therapist and client.

Usually women therapists in mental health clinics and counseling centers are rated as more understanding but outcome statistics favor neither female nor male therapists to any reliable extent.[6] However, "professional patients," if we may call them that, often have very strong opinions about therapists and culturally resemble the therapists themselves (being protestant or Jewish and not Catholic, being upper middle class and well educated, as well as "psychologically sophisticated" persons). These similarities between therapists and patients has given rise to the YAVIS syndrome: young, attractive, verbal, intelligent, and successful. No wonder the lower class patients, or potential patients, suffer more mental hardships and are more in need of help: Therapists cater to those similar to themselves. And most therapists are young (for a while, at least), attractive, verbal, intelligent, and successful. Like chooses like. The analyst's couches are full of the YAVIS types; and if not any longer young, certainly the other four criteria are met,with the "successful" category being important enough to afford psychoanalysis at the rate for 3 to 6 times a week where the fee is often well above $75 per hour. No lower class persons with their anguishing needs can subscribe to the analyst's regimen; few would understand what the analyst was talking about; and few analysts, even if they could get the fees, would treat the lower class psychologically unprepared and unsophisticated client/patient.

The language of therapy in the psychoanalytic framework is also of vast importance. The kind of secret code of the analyst is, itself, a power move: To label the person, to render his/her attributes (symptoms) as abnormal or atypical, or to reduce the importance of what the person says, feels or does as not itself genuine but as representing an offshoot of the label given the patient. One often thinks, and observes, that clinicians, and especially "depth" clinicians, do not accept people at face value in consistent ways, but see people as conglomerates of symptoms, defenses, and other unattractive attributes. With such apparently negative ways of looking at potential patients and actual patients, how can the patient as a human being enter into this kind of derogatory framework with any prospect of being respected, helped or understood?[7] One has to be very "sick" to qualify for psychoanalysis — but also have the other positive attributes that make one a "good patient" — but the ones most in need of help (the lower social classes) are seldom treated, and the ones treated are already the most successful in life. What makes up "success" means one has climbed the socioeconomic ladder and is able to buy the services of the psychoanalyst irrespective of need.

The matter of transference and countertransference comes into muddy the treatment situation even more. Transference is a technical term used very loosely by most therapists, pscyhoanalytic or otherwise, and refers to the literal transference of the client's earlier life problems onto the therapist, a curious matter on the face of it since the psychoanalytic therapist is supposed to be impartial, objective, and emotionally noninvolved. The way this impasse was solved by Freud was to say that the transference phenomenon is due to the patient "transferring" both positive and negative feelings from significant people in earlier life onto the therapist during treatment. The big problem here is that the "transference" has to be "analyzed" out of existence, which is to say it has to be put in the right perspective as not belonging to the therapist at all but as defensively derived from the patient's past. It takes a long time to resolve the transference and this makes treatment last a long, long time. It is not necessary to go into the alleged number of types of transference phenomenon; one is enough! But the undoing becomes the problem for the patient and, of course, insures the psychoanalyst that the patient will be around for a while. In spite of the alleged objectivity of the therapist, a matter of "countertransference" comes up — the tendency of the *therapist* (the psychoanalyst) to be emotional, positive or negative, about the patient. Now we really have problems in therapy! All this countertransference occurs despite the fact that the patient does not know the analyst and cannot match informational input and evaluation of or toward the analyst comparable to the analyst's knowledge of the patient (who is revealing his/her innermost life to the therapist). One can readily see what a jumble of alleged influences and interactions are posited as characterizing the psychoanalytic framework. A potential patient entering into this mishmash of hypothetical interactions with his/her psychoanalyst, especially in view of the fact that analysis is very costly of time, money, and emotional involvement — in the absence of any proof of the superiority of psychoanalytic therapy over the shorter-term therapies — would seemingly have to have more substantial reasons for such an undertaking. Or just be unmindful of what was to come owing to reacting to a stereotype of a hearsay nature about psychoanalysis.

Analysts are very selective in their choice of patients. One cannot just call up a psychoanalyst, get an appointment and begin therapy. In my studies at the Washington School of Psychiatry, part of which course was to "be analyzed," I called many psychoanalysts for appointments; few would even see me on a provisional basis although I was already trained as a Ph.D. level (clinical and child) psychologist and was a student at the WSP. There was, as is commonly known, a prejudice against taking in psychologists for training — although the WSP was then more liberal than most psychoanalytic training and educational centers — but many other matters entered in also. For example, figuring importantly were degree of disturbance, anxiousness in daily living, and willingness to submit to the rather rigorous regimen of treatment prescribed (many of the WSP psychiatrists would allow two, three, or four visits per week, rather than require the more orthodox regimen of five or six hours per week — even the analyst wants some time off!) And, probably, just whether the analyst felt the potential patient would be a "good patient" on some more or less subjective basis. In a very early study of about 2,000 patients at the Berlin Psychoanalytic Institute, during a decade between the two World Wars, only about 15 to 16 percent of these patients were finally accounted for on a follow-up basis as to their "success" in psychoanalytic psychotherapy.[8] It is difficult, of course, to keep track of people once they have left treatment, but in such a formidable undertaking as that of the BPI one might hope that patients were better kept track of and more especially since many had therapy lasting into the hundreds of hours. One other significant feature of the BPI is that of the 2,000-odd persons applying for help, less than half entered treatment (the remaining half was screened out, or didn't choose to go on, or were interrupted in their plans for other reasons); hence the availability of psychoanalytic or psychodynamic treatment even among these select people is low.

Women have had a particularly difficult time with psychoanalysis.[9] In the first instance, Freudian psychology is very sexist, assigning to women "penis envy" of the male and other emotional attributes that separate them from males and make them into second class patients for a variety of reasons; perhaps even second class human beings as women have been viewed as "more emotional" than men and thereby unreliable in responsible roles in life. "An hysterical woman can ruin any office," as one male therapist put it. In everyday parlance women, as we well know, are given short shrift: "If we can find a good woman candidate, we'll run her for office," one politician was quoted as saying. Substitute "man" for "woman" in both of those quotes and one can see how prejudiced and ridiculous each statement is. But psychoanalysis has not overcome these common social prejudices against women, incorporating many of them into the fabric of psychoanalysis and covering these assignments with emotionally-laden, technical terms, thereby seeming to make the description valid.

In a resume of some of the stereotypes applied to women in psychoanalytic therapy, Tennov[10] (1976, pp. 92-100) covers the following: encouraging and stressing guilt feelings; blaming the patient for dependency yet seeming to encourage it; holding the woman in therapy by use of vague threats as to what would happen if therapy were stopped; failure to refer women out to other resources when therapy did not progress well; alleging that women presented biased pictures of their lives, lacking objectivity; failure of therapist to recognize the nature of the household/family problems and settings in which women live and operate; stressing sexual content out of proportion to other problems; holding and expressing patriarchal values; being cold and unsupportive of women; and sometimes failing to respect confidential information. Women had their reactions to these types of therapeutic handling: Becoming overly dependent upon the male therapist; being unduly influenced in life decisions (marriage, schooling, career, etc.) by the male therapist's expressed opinions; lack of encouragement for trying to help oneself; and tending to feel isolated from other women during the time in therapy. While we cannot assign causality or blame to the therapist of any persuasion for all of this array of female restrictions to therapy, the overall viewpoint of psychoanalytic/psychodynamic therapy suggests these biases, at least according to reports received from women who have had extensive psychoanalytic therapy.

Within the psychoanalytic ranks, women analysts also rebelled (somewhat and not always consistently) against the traditional Freudian view of women. One can count among these women some outstanding examples: Melitta Schmidelbert, Karen Horney; Frieda Fromm-Reichman; Helen Deutsch; Jean Baker Miller; Charlotte Wolff; and others; albeit not all of these stand for the same criticisms of Freudian psychotherapy and/or its implications for women in treatment or out.[11] The percentage of male versus female psychiatrists and psychologists helps support the male viewpoint, whether the male clinicians are psychoanalytic or not. In the 1970s roughly 75 to 90 percent of all psychiatrists and psychologists doing psychotherapy (not necessarily Freudian psychotherapy) were males; it would be surprising if most of them did not hold to male and female stereotypes, holding reservations about women becoming socially and professionally prepared and assertive, giving up or reducing their domestic roles, and becoming active politically. If psychotherapists — psychoanalytic or not — hold to the traditional male/female stereotypes, they are likely to translate some of these stereotypes into therapeutic attitudes and practices, some of which were recounted above.[12] While the percentage of women psychologically and psychiatrically trained psychotherapists is on the increase, women still fail to hold the higher reaches of the profession at university posts, in clinical directorships, and the like. We cannot blame this condition on any psychotherapy viewpoint, but the professions, controlled by men, have helped keep women in the more minor and dependent roles assigned to them traditionally, and this attitude is more supported by psychoanalytic viewpoints than most people are ready to admit. If one, then, enters psychodynamic/psychoanalytic therapy as a cause celebre, it is most likely, whether one is man or a woman, that the more traditional viewpoints concerning women will be espoused; and if they are not openly espoused, they will likely be tacitly present in the exchanges between therapist and patient.

BEHAVIORAL THERAPIES

Behavioral therapies have grown at an exponential rate over the past two or three decades and show promise — if one can call it that — of absorbing the psychotherapy field amost completely in due time. Historically the behavioral viewpoint grew from at least three main sources: From the work of Skinner and associates, beginning as early as the 1930s and continuing on to more open applications to psychotherapy and the changing of behavior among handicapped populations, in the 1950s; from the work of Eysenck, in England, who may have been the first to use, publicly at least, the term "behavior therapy"; and to the work of Wolpe, first in South Africa and later in the USA, Wolpe being the first full-fledged therapist himself among these leaders to develop and use what later was called behavior therapy.[13]

Skinner's viewpoint is characterized by the term "operant behavior," and refers to how the organism's behavior is shaped by its consequences in the environment, how it operates on and is affected by the environmental exchange between the organism and the environment. Operant behavior stresses positive reinforcement; while this is the hallmark of operant behavior methods, many other concepts and operations are part of the operant framework. It is not useful here to try to give a full explanation of how operant behavior is experimentally based and how wide are its applications. Operant methods taught clinicians, teachers, and other experimentalists how to arrange the environment and the consequences of the person's behavior so that change in a desired direction would more likely take place. Take, for example, the behavior of a retarded youngster in school. Teachers are known — as are parents — to exhort the child to earn to do some simple thing like eating with a fork, tying a shoelace, dressing, and so forth. Exhortation and random trial-and-error do not usually produce much results in such instances. However, arranging the environment so that the child approaches the matter of using a fork, as an example, consists of first teaching the child how to hold the fork, how to spear a small piece of meat, how to use the fork to cut small pieces of some food, and so on. As the child approaches these matters, and succeeds, reinforcement occurs: The food is tasty, the parent or the teacher praises the child by saying, "That is very good — now let's try it again," and so on; so that gradually over time the child begins to show some modest skill in this fairly complex set of behaviors. Similarly, a retarded child may be taught to put on and take off a shirt or slipover sweater, use a zipper or buttons for fastening, and so forth. The successive approximations route is followed — one step at a time, generously reinforced with continued setting of graduated tasks, leading to a more complex series of acts that complete an integrated whole (feeding oneself, dressing and undressing, lacing shoes, and so forth). These procedures can be extended to any behavior whatsoever, from simple acts like those just mentioned out to learning to read and concentrate, do arithmetic, and perhaps print or write. No task that can be defined adequately can fail to come under some behavioral control and success engendered insofar as the task is relevant to the child's capacities. Sometimes the child is extended far beyond what was originally thought to be the capacity for given behaviors — many retarded children have learned a host of self-care, cooperative, social, educational, and other behaviors under the guidance and expert care of operantly trained psychologists, teachers, parents, and others.[14]

The success of operant behavioral methods with handicapped and retarded children (and, to some extent, adults) lead in time to the application of these methods to more normal persons and to psychotherapy cases. In psychotherapy, for example, behavioral methods have improved the delineation of the problem(s) areas to be investigated and changed, have helped wives and husbands more able settle their differences and work on stronger points between them, have helped parents resolve or greatly ameliorate difficulties with their children, have instructed classroom teachers how better to help all children — handicapped or not — learn better. And no other therapy in the history of the profession has accumulated so many striking successes with traditionally refractory problems and no therapy has been applied so widely to a range of problems from the lowly handicapped child in an institution out to the most sophisticated adult who wants to stop smoking, lose weight, have a better relationship with a spouse, reduce tension on the job, learn to concentrate better in academic and professional ways, and to gain higher levels of social skills. The reasons for these successes are manifold, as one might know, but the perseverence in tackling problems and finding new ways to view old problems, has characterized the behavior modification (or behavior change) profession so thoroughly that its successes have become almost pro forma. That does not mean that all problems fall easily before the behavior modification expert; on the contrary, many areas so far yield grudgingly to any therapeutic effort (stopping smoking, e.g.), but the behavioral movement has produced the most versatile ways of tackling these refractory areas and has better kept track of its successes and failures in ways altogether exemplary in the history of psychology broadly and in the history of psychotherapy more specifically. The revolution began by Skinner in the second and third decades of this century, first at Harvard, later at the Universities of Minnesota and Indiana, then again at Harvard, is unmatched in the history of psychology and will doubtlessly remain so for some time to come.

The work of Eysenck[15] and others, in England, is more indirect, less experimental and less clinical in origin. Eysenck had the foresight and insight (to put some stress on fairly nonbehavioral formulations for the sake of immediate intelligibility) to see how behavioral methods were more scientifically defensible, turned in better results when utilized, formulated problems in ways that allowed them to be researched and modified, and showed how training and education of not only experts but lay users of behavioral methods could be accomplished. His ability to write cogently and persuasively about how behavioral methods worked over a wide range of problems was particularly potent in the 1950s, 60s, and 70s, when he challenged the pat versions of psychoanalytic (and other "depth-oriented" psychotherapies) and their alleged successes.[16] He brought therapists, personality theorists, clinicians, educators, and others out of the intellectual doldrums of supposing that depth measures were the only ways to deal with human distress, neurosis, and the like by showing how traditional therapies (going back long before behavioral therapy methods were extant) could hardly do better than chance improvements among patient populations and by challenging therapists to show that what they alleged they did was really accomplished. Eysenck was, and remains, an expert researcher who knew how to ask searching and provocative questions and how to bring scientific evidence to bear on the answers.

Joseph Wolpe[17] who, although trained in medicine and was/is a psychiatrist, writes, thinks, acts, and does research like a psychologist (Skinner and Eysenck are both psychologists), many people would say. He formulated some very far-reaching observations clinically – based on experimental research with animals – about psychotherapy which have held up to this time and which have ramified into a variety of treatment directions. Wolpe's position was based more on classical conditioning, Pavlovian conditioning, insofar as learning theory and experimental psychology are concerned; contrasted with Skinner who developed, described and utilized more a nonclassical, respondent conditioning model, known as operant conditioning. Wolpe made an important contribution when he formulated the "reciprocal inhibition" model for psychotherapy. He noted that one cannot be both relaxed and anxious simultaneously, a matter we have all known in a naive sense, to be sure; but to couple these opposites for treatment purposes led to a strong emphasis on relaxation techniques (some adapted from Jacobson), on desensitization, and on anxiety management in general. In the later case – anxiety management – Wolpe constructed and utilized what is known as the anxiety hierarchy, related to fears and phobias. This is a list of provocative situations, starting with the least harmful, and progressively coming to "home base," to the most dreaded of circumstances, a ladder or hierarchy of influence on the person as s/he encounters, or thinks about, the troublesome events. Suppose a person has a phobia for elevators and cannot bear the thought of doing shopping in stores where elevators are commonly used, even necessary. Not to be able to shop widely and freely is, in our day and time, a debilitating matter. Tackling this problem through psychoanalysis is almost futile because it would not provide any ways and mean to grapple *directly with the problem but would tend to set it aside as a symptom of, or derivative from, an allegedly more basic problem* which would, in characteristic psychoanalytic style, have to be pursued over time. The assumption in the latter case being that as the person wrestled with and overcame basic personality problems and defects, these specific fears and phobias would melt away. However, that has never been demonstrated as a useful therapeutic tactic. What Wolpe did was different but very commonsensical now that we know it and can see its plausability.

Wolpe instructed the patient to construct a hierarchy of provocative (anxiety provoking) situations (from least to most) in relation to the elevator. What would be the *least* anxiety producing in connection with a possible visit to a department stores where the elevator would have to be used? The patient constructed the following hierarchy; from least to most:

Looking around the house to see what purchases were needed from a store;
Noting that groceries, bed linens, and childrens' clothing were needed;
Arranging to meet friend for lunch before shopping;
Thinking of being in restaurant where shopping was to be done;
Finishing the lunch and deciding on where to shop first;

Doing some grocery shopping on the first floor;
Finishing this shopping, taking stairs to second floor to buy bed linens;
Realizing childrens' clothing was on the fifth floor with no stairs available;
Walking across the first floor of department store toward the elevator;
Approaching the elevator (within 50 feet); seeing people get on and off elevator as it was approached;
Waiting for elevator to return so as to enter;
Walking into open elevator;
Being pushed about with crowd entering elevator;
Door of elevator closing and moving upward.

What good, one may ask, is there in listing all these things when one knows them already? One does know them in a kind of inarticulate sense, but there is great value in listing them and in arousing the feelings, the emotional responses, that are connected thereto. What Wolpe identified as most salient was taking each step in the hierarchy toward the more anxiety laden end point and talking about the anxiety aroused. Let us say the patient reported that as she finished lunch, her anxiety began to be felt as she knew she was now through with the preliminaries and was going to do her shopping, eventually having to cope with the elevator phobia in order to get to the fifth floor. At the point in the hierarchy related to finishing lunch, the therapist and patient would stop and talk about this juncture; the patient would do some deep breathing and as she let out the air say to herself, "I will be able to cope with this anxiety, even though it is difficult at first," or equivalent statements. This particular step may be settled on, so to say, for several trials with the deep-breathing and until the patient is ready to move on to the next step. That next step, too, is expected to be anxiety arousing inasmuch as it is a step closer to the phobic situation; one would have to settle in on this second anxiety-provoking phase to some extent. And so on through the whole hierarchy. The patient might go through this hierarchy on several occasions before actually going to the store (called the *in vivo* part) and trying out her anxiety and phobic controlling efforts.

Peoples' phobias may be subdivided into different length hierarchies; once a hierarchy is established, experience with it vicariously may lead to more differentiation. But all the while the patient is becoming active, coping, structuring, and planful about the anxiety and about the specific anxiety producing situation. The hierarchy is not always a set matter, it may lengthen or shorten with experience. As one enters the real life situation, the hierarchy may be greatly shortened and one may, alone, run through the hierarchy before going shopping to bring matters under control without the therapist's help. The objective, is of course, to do-it-oneself and be able to dispense with the therapist as soon as the tact is understood and proven to be a productive matter.

The patient gains in self-control throughout. The patient makes the hierarchy, delineates the steps, goes through the hierarchy vicariously with the therapist (at first), checks it out against reality, practices the self-control inherent in using the hierarchy at any time during the day (it is not confined to the therapist's office), and so forth. How much more salutary this is than exploring in a vague, general, and rambling way what might have caused one in his/her younger years to be phobic toward elevators; and especially to find out that one did not actually experience elevators as such until one was 18, so the elevator phobia must have been related to some other — usually parentally related — event or series of events, the discovery of which, the relevance of which — assuming some discovery and relevance were possible — would have to be ascertained over a lengthy period of time. In the meanwhile as one would be searching for the elevator phobia beginning point in the psychoanalytic mode, one would continue to avoid elevators, be anxious at the thought of shopping or attending theater or parking one's car where elevators were involved, all the more *reinforcing the avoidance* of the elevator phenomenon, thereby solidifying it, very likely. In this avoidance model, albeit part of the psychoanalytic method of coping, one would be increasing the phobia, not decreasing; one would be playing helpless, so to say, in the face of the phobia rather than in assertive efforts toward conquering it. One has to learn to cope with the situation, qua situation, in the case of any phobia, fear, or apprehension, not back off and search for another, indirect route to the problem, unless that indirect route is clearly related to the goal. Since the goal of psychoanalysis is mostly making the unconscious conscious, understanding one's psyche, reliving childhood experiences, and so forth, these have the most tenuous connection with the current event one needs help with when approaching a therapist. The best way to tackle a problem is to tackle it, to plan an approach, to assert oneself in the effort to overcome the distressful situation; that's the way we usually solve problems — so why not parsimoniously do the same thing in relation to the more difficult problems? It takes more effort to be sure, but it is already "in our repertoire" as the behavioral therapist would say — we already know how to do it (enter and leave an elevator), having done it in other situations — so the preliminaries are in order and have only to be shaped to meet the present set of exigencies.

The contributions of Wolpe, then, were highly clinically-related, directly applicable in therapy, and paid good dividends. They have been refined and extended, and combined, and reshaped, and so forth over the years, but the essential model is still useful and productive. Many people who are only beginning to note they might be developing a phobia — say, someone who is afraid to get back into his/her car after an accident — could practice these relaxation/desensitization measures on his/her own; or consult a therapist adept in helping the patient with the hierarchy, if that move seemed indicated, and get on with overcoming the difficulty. One graduate student clinician of mine encountered a client who had a "car driving phobia" and this client was helped by the graduate student with *in vivo* instruction in overcoming the phobia. They went to the parking lot where the car was parked (having been driven in and parked by the man's wife as they both attended school together). And as they walked closer to the lot the client would voice his concern and anxiety about the car, they would stop and talk about it, then move on, and so on, constructing, so to say, a hierarchy based not on the memory or thoughts about the situation but the actual pathway to the car in the parking lot. In a few sessions the client was able to sit in the car — in the passenger front seat — then in the driver's seat and, in time to start up the car, move it forth and back in the parking lot, later in an unused school parking lot near his home, then finally getting on the road to drive the car as he had before the accident. How would an analyst approach this problem? Would the analyst disclaim the importance of the accident and credit some childhood kind of experience (maybe a car accident, possibly, or some other type of disaster presumably psychologically similar or equivalent) and seek relief that way? Or would the analyst probe the "meaning of the car," "the meaning of being helpless in not driving," the "meaning associated with depending so completely on his wife since he had been such an assertive adequate person vis-a-vis her and women generally," or some other such formulation. The analyst has his heyday, so to say when he/she can avoid the *specifics* of a person's problem and try to approach the issues in the general, probing, history-seeking, transference-related way, and not be contested easily; because, until Wolpe and the other behavioral therapists came along, there was no direct challenge — except common sense and our daily life experiences which were not given enough credit — to the psychoanalytic model. The young man with the "car phobia" was able to drive again in about three months, following short weekly sessions in therapy, built primarily on a successive approximations model of tackling directly the anxiety provoking situation.

If one looks into the content of behavior therapy books one encounters references to an abundance of techniques designed to tackle certain kinds or classes or problems people present. There is not a highly specific set of answers awaiting each and every person with each and every problem, like a dictionary or cookbook set of prescriptions, but there are a variety of techniques of possible practical benefit to classes of problems. For example one could find several techniques for helping students experiencing difficulty concentrating on their studies or when reading; on helping students set up work/sleep/study schedules that allow them to use their time more productively; on helping shy and awkward students develop more competent social skills so that they can speak more freely with others, ask for dances, dates, coke breaks and the like and become generally more socially adept. As to phobic persons — phobias of a long-standing nature being one of the most difficulty therapeutic areas to tackle — one could work out a number of *in vivo* tactics to help, in addition to vicariously setting up hierarchies and engaging in systematic desensitization. One can develop techniques for helping parents deal with recalcitrant children or help teachers with the same problem in the classroom; and so on through any list of common problems people experience from early childhood out to senility.

It might be apparent by now that behavioral methods are often a quick-response type of therapy quite consonant with all kinds of short-term psychotherapy and, indeed, most behavioral therapy is short-term. The preventive value of an alert, up-front, problem-solving therapy is at once obvious. Therapeutic teams can and do exist in schools, in businesses, in corporations, for early on identification of problems of various types — from temper outbursts among team members working cooperatively on a project — out to bosses who interact aversively with the employees. If a thousand people in a given factory or corporate office need some kind of help, how effective, efficient, timely would psychoanalysis be, or, indeed, any psychodynamically-oriented therapy with its cumbersome set of assumptions, requirements for therapeutic participation, and so on, not to mention the fact that there are not enough therapists to even get started with such a large clientele. Twenty-five behavioral therapists could, once the problem situation had been surveyed and the proper baselines established, offer help to the 1,000 employees in our hypothetical corporation, first by setting up small group discussion formats — with, say, 10 persons per group x 25 therapists, each working with 4 groups, perhaps each meeting for a couple of hours once a week — and offer more mental health instruction (call it therapy, too, if you wish) in a month or two than all the analysts in New York, Washington, D.C., Chicago, San Francisco, and Los Angeles combined over a several year period. If economy — cost/effectiveness — is important (which it surely is), then the behavioral approach is of inestimable value. Even if ten percent of the 1,000 hypothetical cases in the corporation need more individual attention, this could be offered by and through the same behavioral trained therapists using individual therapy where needed, or arranging for family participation where indicated. The flexibility of the behavioral approach would be a very large plus; moreover it would combine the resources of all participants — client, therapists, company policies, etc. — in one aggregate effort that would be far more comprehensive than the one-at-a-time-in-depth procedures of the psychoanalysts.

In the last decade or so, attention to possible "deteriorating effects" from psychotherapy (and from psychoanalysis) has been brought forward.[18] Freud saw the struggle between negative and positive influences in one's life and attributed its effects to disturbing the delicate balance which does not (may not) get restated, thus the person deteriorates. Possibly, too, a kind of therapy that promotes too much introspection, without showing one the way out of the mentalistic impasses, might add to the person's stress and confuse further.[19] It is important, of course, to know early on if some deteriorating or deleterious outcome is anticipated and switch the person to a different therapist, use a different method, lean out the number of sessions so the client is not kept on the "therapy hot seat" so long, and/or possibly recommending stopping therapy for the nonce. If a short-term, behavior approach is utilized, one can tell pretty soon how the client is likely to react and whether progress can be expected;

after a few sessions in the case of suspected deterioration, a change can be instituted. The likelihood of barreling along without due regard to how the client is faring is more likely with a depth therapy than with a behavioral approach simply because it is integral to the latter to know how, where, what, when, etc. everything is going on with the patient; thus changes can be made in a more timely fashion than with the passive, exploratory, mentalistic emphasis found in psychoanalysis. It should not be forgotten that short of actual deterioration of the client as discussed above, the problem of wasting the client's time and money is much more common and should be addressed early on by all clients going into therapy of any type whatsoever. Again, if a short-term framework is adhered to, the chances of discovering any sets of influences — good, bad or indifferent — are more likely than with the longer-term approaches that fail to monitor the patient carefully and well.

TOWARD A MORE SOCIAL BEHAVIORISM

As already indicated, behavioral methods grew first out of the experimental laboratory, especially the operant conditioning influence. Wolpe's ideas, also, grew out of Pavlovian conditioning. As behavioral methods became applied more and more to a wider range of clinical problems, the social matrix, the far-reaching social influences, began to be more and more recognized. Although the social movement got mixed in with cognitive influences (which will be dealt with below), there were enough social influences in dealing with a variety of handicapped children in their school, home, and peer settings, to cause behavior modification researchers and practitioners to consider more and more openly the social arrangements which people are embedded in ways in which the social setting becomes part of the issue of environmental control. It is not enough to say that the behavior problems of school children are thus and so in some lower class setting versus how children of the same age behave in upper middle class settings. If discipline is more difficult to establish, owing to natural social norms in the lives of lower class children, then somewhat different classroom structures, contingency management regimens, peer influence and support, and the like will need to be thought of and tried out compared to handling (say) disciplinary problems among the middle class children. Parental instruction about child development and the normal problems of children will need to be approached differently when aimed at different social/economic classes. However, the essential core of behavioral techniques will be used in the sense of contingency management, reinforcement principles, how, and why punishment is probably not recommended, and so forth.

As behavioral influence techniques came to be more and more widely used, there grew up a range of techniques suitable to each area of application. In dealing with marital issues, the range of behavioral techniques would differ in some ways from what one would use in parent-child conflicts and differently from those used among homosexual couples living together, or among phobia cases, and so on. However, in all these topological differences, the hard core — so to say — of *behavioral principles* would be the basis of the particular choice of intervention techniques among the wide-ranging problem areas.

It became increasingly clear in time that much of what we call pathology, or behavioral pathology, was more fundamentally a matter of social skill.[20] This observation was most clearly realized among high school, college, and young adult populations, many of whom came for psychotherapy because they felt socially estranged, inadequate, and reported serious lacks in social confidence. (We have already referred, above, to some of the range of socially-related problems found among two hundred late adolescent and young adult applicants to a university counseling center.) In response to these social skill types of problems, behavior change efforts proliferated; in a decade or more, dozens of books and hundreds of articles, not to mention dozens of "social skill packages" for training people in more adequate interpersonal relations, appeared on the scene. The social skills area was a "natural" for the behavioral intervention expert. Even among traditional therapists, lacking training in both social skills techniques and behavioral methods, the recommendation for social competence became more clearly recognized, thus supporting, indirectly, the social skills movement as a behavioral area. Small groups related to dating problems, conversational problems, handling anger, dealing with moodiness, overcoming shyness, and so on, almost endlessly, began to arise in setting where youthful applicants for psychological help appeared.

The last point is particularly important: People came for help asking for individual therapy, but their problem areas related to social skill. How could these people be best treated? People with concentration and self-management/discipline problems often go to therapists for individual treatment. Is it not possible that a significant number of these socially-related competence or skill problems belong more accurately in the area of social skills training? And would not the best first approach be to tackle this range of social skills problems, especially those involving the opposite sex, in small groups where the members shared common problems and common lacks in competence? I have argued elsewhere that social skills training is probably the preferred approach to a large variety of problems of adolescents and youth, and that individual therapy, albeit sometimes preferred or even necessary, can often take place after the social competency problems are improved upon. People react individually to social skills issues with depression, discouragement, hostility, prejudice, and sometimes develop serious problems in other areas (excessive use of drugs and alcohol). The zeroing in on social lacks, felt or observed, can sometime short-circuit otherwise lengthy therapy and give the person more confidence in his actual relationships with others, and better understanding as to how he malfunctions in relation to felt or actual injury. There is some literature that supports this latter point — start with and emphasize social skills before engaging in individual therapy — and the matters concerned with this viewpoint are being more steadily examined.[21]

COGNITIVE BEHAVIORAL INFLUENCES

In the early and middle 1970s a few psychologists began writing about and researching "cognitive behavioral" matters. They felt that behavioral methods, theory and practice, stemming from Skinner, Wolpe, Eysenck, and others was too narrow and that the perspective of the individual had to be taken more directly into consideration. It was sometimes noticed that behavioral intervention methods would start action on some behavioral complaint area, per se, without taking into consideration more fully how the patient saw (perceived) and understood and evaluated the problem. *The* problem had been the behavioral difficulty itself — say, for example, a child's bed-wetting — and intervention and remedial efforts had taken the problem too superficially and not given enough consideration to the child's emotional state, his/her perspective, and so forth. While this criticism may apply in some cases, it is probably poor behavioral intervention — as it would be poor therapy in medicine or any other problem-solving area — to just jump in and try to change something before one knew what the larger issues were. All therapists would agree, I believe, that any stated problem is not the whole problem, and that often there is a penumbra of other difficulties, or even a core of difficulties, that are not expressed well by the *named* problem. Anyhow, the cognitive movement drew more and more attention to the presumably larger issues and to how the client or patient felt, saw, emoted to, the expressed (or named) problem. More emphasis came to be placed on the cognitive issues. Now the young, the handicapped, immature, retarded, autistic, disturbed child, as well as many other patients/clients, do not have much to say, cognitively speaking. It is natural that methods first developed with the (mostly available) handicapped populations on which some important branches of behavior modification first exerted their efforts would not show a lot of cognitive elements. Verbal methods of inquiry — asking question of these essentially seriously deficit persons — would lead nowhere, and better data would be derived from close, careful, consistent, and contingent observation. In the early heyday of behavioral methods, the most available patients/clients were in institutions, and the most pressing problems of social living were there; the combination of newly emerging techniques, available and needy populations, combined to give a great and important impetus to behavioral methods.

Not only were the cited populations ready, willing, and available to behavioral interventions, these interventions tackled problems not previously undertaken, and results were generally encouraging. When one hits "pay dirt" in this manner, one doesn't give a lot of credence to some other, possibly more subtle, even more elusive problems at the outset. Perhaps these wider considerations should have grown more robust early on — but they didn't. Furthermore, school populations of essentially normal youth and young adults also were in need of help.

Commensurate with the growth of behavioral methods was the enormous growth of community mental health clinics throughout the USA, beginning with the mid-1940s, and going on at a high rate until the late 1970s. Other programs in hospitals, where a new emphasis arose in attempts to get people out of this institutional setting; teaching more and better self-care — even though often supported or supplemented by drug treatments — began to burgeon as a social, economic, and institutional need. Behavioral methods were ideal for all of these problem areas. The versatility of behavioral methods was also shown in coupling its resources with the various parental movements in support of all kinds of handicapped children, beginning with the 1950s and gaining momentum with each passing year, hitting a plateau in the early 1980s when political changes depressed all kinds of educational, social, and vocational help to the handicapped (as well as other needy groups). With these highly encouraging growth areas for behavioral methods and techniques, not much was learned about the later-to-come developments called "cognitive behavior modification." Perhaps the groundwork had first to be laid by the more or less direct applications from the laboratory to the field, the clinic, and the school settings. When real gains were demonstrated by the first waves of technical competence, by the handling of old problems anew, and by the tackling of heretofore unmet needs, the behavioral movement had enough fish to fry to keep it busy for decades.

Some would contest the amount of contributions from cognitive behavioral efforts. Applications to depression seem promising; self-control measures and self-management techniques appear sometimes to be enhanced with some emphasis on cognitive variables.[22] But all communication, verbal or not, has to exist in the exchange between persons, in the clinic or outside, whether sets of instructions, examples, modeling opportunities (as communications) are mainly extensions of the behavioral data base or not; and whether something in this emphasis new and different has really appeared, only time will tell. Certainly there is no disputing the avalanche of change brought on by the behavioral movement as discussed above; how much the cognitive emphasis has accomplished seems to be moot at this time, although the advertising and ballyhoo for cognitive interventions seem to go on unabated. No matter how a therapist attempts to help a person, by whatever range of techniques, the bottom line always has to be some answer to the question: Did the behavior change? If so, how, to what extent, at what cost, under what auspices, under what conditions? and the like. Even if one alleges that one's feelings and outlook on him/herself and on life have changed, there is some data to back it up, some behavioral change: "I am not depressed in the mornings when I get up," "I enjoy parties and other get-togethers more than I did," "I feel more confident when I undertake a new effort or a new relationship," and so on.

There are always some specifics that one notes, in assigning improvement, and that means some identifiable behavior change. The cognitive behavioral movement would gain credence, then, insofar as it shows broader ways to tackle problems, more originality in problem-solving, broader based than the (already numerous) ways to change behavior from the repertoires of behavioral changers over the past two or three decades. The modest look at psychotherapy is that it is useful, that this can produce some changes in people, that the various theories of therapy are more alike than different, and that the innovations — if they are that — from cognitive approaches really, simply, fit in with the changes already ongoing; and that no new miracles have been wrought. On the whole, the behavioral movement is more versatile, more efficient and effective (costs less), and embraces sets of techniques and philosophies that are usable by parents, teachers, probation officers, special education experts, in-office clinicians, and so forth, far more convincingly than has any therapy in the past (or in the present). The situation with behavioral interventions as a broad approach to human psychological and social difficulties is a bit like that of putting more fluoride in the water to prevent tooth decay. If communities have sufficient amounts of fluoride in their water supply, it has been shown that dental caries and other problems are reduced; it does not mean that you can take a child who is beginning to have dental problems and douse him/her with fluoride-treated water and have the tooth problems disappear. Most change efforts in the social, health, and psychological fields are broad-based and do not rise or fall on individual treatment alone, although behavioral methods have a good record in this regard (e.g., with all kinds of handicapped persons).

HOW PSYCHOTHERAPY SERVICE DELIVERY SYSTEMS FIT IN

Recently there has developed a sizeable data base put together by the present writer and students on how clients/patients flow through a clinic, in short, how service delivery takes place.[23] People apply to a clinic for some mental health service — usually psychotherapy — in community mental health clinics, in counseling centers in universities and colleges and in private psychological/psychiatric clinics. This application begins with an introduction, usually, called the "intake interview." This intake, for short, gathers information from the client, addresses issues related to how therapy would take place, tells the prospective client how the clinic (or therapy) works, and address the general issue of whether this is the best place for the client to receive help. Referral out in some cases might take place.

Presently available norms — and these are extensive norms — based on millions of patients/clients, from hundreds of clinics, throughout the USA —

indicate that the average number of psychotherapy visits ranges primarily from four to eight. Sometimes, in private settings, in contrast to clinics run by communities or universities, the average number of sessions will range up to eight or so. *But the national norms, from all sources, is clearly short-term psychotherapy.*

These therapy delivery systems are characterized by a variety of therapists – psychologists, social workers, psychiatrists – and by a variety of viewpoints (behavioral, psychodynamic, humanistic, nondirective, and so on). It appears strongly that regardless of the clients (children, adults, adolescents, families, groups) that the average number of sessions is about the same. The vastness and the stability of the average number of sessions – broadly speaking, from 4 to 8 – is so compelling and so important that it has to figure in our present discussion about psychotherapy.

A second important fact about the beginning point in therapy – the intake interview – is that about one-half of the clients who come to a clinic do not come back again (for therapy) at that time. They may come again months or years later, or they may go to another clinic (at any one time, about one-quarter to one-third of the applications to a given clinic have had some previous psychotherapy). What has been called "dropping out" of treatment – the more technical and better descriptive term is "attrition" – has been studied only unsystematically in the research literature pertaining to psychotherapy. The most information about attrition has been contained in three general reviews in the technical literature, some shorter reviews plus the present research by myself and my students.

A third characteristic of how people utilize a psychotherapy opportunity is that the attrition curve shows a characteristic slope, that is, people continue to "leave the system" in smaller and smaller numbers, so that, as time goes by, fewer and fewer clients remain in therapy. Some (about 8 to 10 percent) continue out to an upper range of over 10 to 15 sessions, but by the fifth to sixth sessions between 60 and 70 percent of the people entering the system have left therapy. The slope of the attrition curve is shown below.

This curve, from intake to the end of therapy, shows that the real phenomenon of psychotherapy is best described by this curve, irrespective of client/patient diagnosis, age, sex, ethnic background, type of treatment, training of the therapist, and so forth. In short, the real hard data on psychotherapy is most inclusively stated by reference to the *attrition curve.* The number of sessions of therapy is uppermost. All else appears secondary.

In some private practice settings – those mainly following a psychoanalytic/psychodynamic viewpoint, the average number of visits may range from 70 or more and into the hundreds of hours. The attrition curve, then, with national averages in the 4 to 8 session range, attest further to the vast differences between psychoanalystic/psychodynamic psychotherapy on the one hand and almost all other therapies on the other hand. This kind of comparison is held to be more rigorous than comparing therapy groups here and there in clinics by

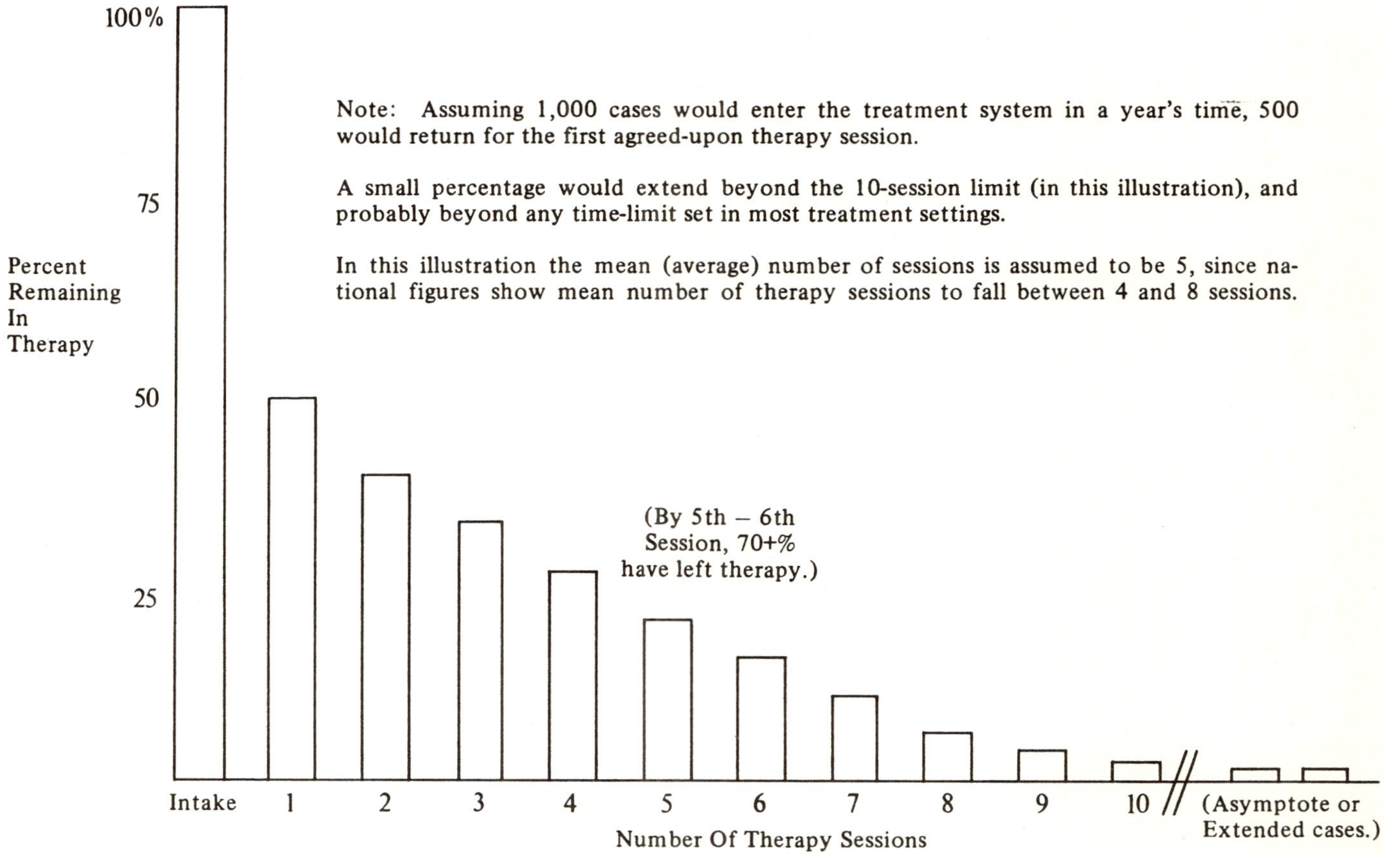

Figure 1. Hypothetical (Smoothed) Version Of The Attrition Curve. Note that of the percent entering the clinic (or the treatment system), about 50 percent come back for the first interview. The declining number continuing to participate in psychotherapy refers to the attrition (or drop-out) rate. This curve has been found in all types of short-term psychotherapy, in psychoanalytic/psychodynamic psychotherapy going into the hundreds of hours, among special problem patients-clients (such as alcoholics, family therapy, phobic cases, individual and group therapy), and among all theories of therapy.

contrasting one method with another (say, behavioral versus psychodynamic; Rogerian versus behavioral and so forth); as the present comparisons in terms of the attrition curve (with the means, standard deviations, and length of the curve (the asymptote) are more robust ways of describing the differences between the therapies. By using the attrition curve one could arrange all possible comparisons between any two or more therapies among the large number extant, and have more meaningful comparisons of how each therapy works in a whole cloth manner than is usually accomplished by present research.

Of what practical importance is the attrition curve finding for the average client about to seek psychotherapy (or to judge what s/he is getting if already in therapy)? And of what value is it to therapists? The answers to these parallel questions — "So what?" — is that there is a lot of meaning for all concerned. If a candidate for therapy knows that on the average most people go to therapy only about a half-dozen times, then that gives a perspective to work from: it does not mean that you, or Mr. Jones, or Ms. Smith will, of necessity, have only that number of visits, but it may mean that, and it may help you to compare yourself in a clearer fashion with others seeking a similar kind of help. If you have a very particular problem — say, e.g., a very persistent phobia — you might need to look at books on the treatment of phobia (see Chapter 8, try to find attrition curves) (good luck!) or try to compare therapists doing different kinds of treatment. The more you know as a consumer — and you are a consumer of an important mental health service — the better choices you can make and the better you can evaluate what you get.

In another context — client evaluation of his/her therapy — what does the attrition curve mean? Does it mean that the average client is "satisfied" with his/her therapy? Or disappointed? Or afraid to go longer in fear of receiving threatening information about oneself? And so on. More information exists that suggests clients are mostly satisfied with their short-term psychotherapy experience rather than not. Budman, Bloom[24] and others have pointed out — as, indeed, we do here — that the *modal* number of visits in outpatient psychotherapy is *one visit* ("modal" refers to the category having the greatest frequency of cases — see "attrition curve" above); that is, more people have just one visit than have two, three, or more visits. Something like 70 to 80 percent of those having only one visit remarked positively (answered questionnaires about their experiences after varying amounts of therapy) about that one visit. If we look, also, at the number of people who apply for, have one visit, in quest of longer-term psychotherapy and/or in quest of psychoanalysis/psychodynamic psychotherapy, we see, here too, that the highest frequency occurs at the first visit, or at the one-visit category. The more long-term psychologists and psychiatrists "weed out" the — to them — less successful or less likely candidates, early on in the application process and also retain only a small percentage of cases that "go the route" to longer-term therapy. So the attrition curve in its various aspects describes pretty accurately how clients and therapists and delivery systems operate in the aggregate. It appears very unlikely that less information than that afforded by the attrition curve is not only very incomplete but may be misleading to both therapists and patients (and prospective patients as well). While studies may be done comparing therapy methods x and y, or y and z, with each other and with controls, the results are often based on patients selected from the attrition curve, we know not where, and results in comparisons, however statistically sophisticated, which lack breadth and representativeness. The ones who leave the therapy for whatever reasons are, perforce, not often retained in the statistics comparing the two methods, and so the final figures may be suspect simply because the attritional impact has greatly changed what has happened along the therapeutic route.

SUMMARY OF PSYCHODYNAMIC AND BEHAVIORAL THERAPIES

In this first of two chapters dealing with the main theories of psychotherapy (see Chapter 4 for further discussion) we have seen many things. The psychodynamic/psychoanalytic theory (or theories) have been the oldest and most prominent viewpoints for decades. Early on in this century and at the end of the 19th century, Freud began to lay down the main postulates and practices of psychoanalysis. While Freud changed his theories somewhat over the years, the essential structure remained the same. Also his dissenters – Jung, Adler, and others – even in their splits with Freud appear to have retained a number of the essentials of psychodynamic/psychoanalytic thinking and practice. The main changes over the decades, especially in the 1940s and later in the works of Fromm, Sullivan, Fromm-Reichman, Horney, and others, moved psychoanalysis more into the social arena while still retaining many features of intrapsychic functioning as a theoretical base and as setting the tasks for analysis in the practical sense.

Psychoanalysis, while often held up to be the modal and preferred form of psychotherapy, has never treated very many people. Modifications of psychoanalysis in the direction of shorter therapies have yielded somewhat on the more orthodox stands taken by Freudians, but the changes appear to have been minor insofar as suggesting a more practical therapy is concerned. Recent efforts to develop short-term, dynamic psychotherapies have also retained the main features of psychoanalytic structure.[25] For example, Sifneos in his discussion of "technique" holds strongly both to traditional psychoanalytic notions by referring to delineating the "underlying psychodynamic" nature of the patients' problems, to selecting patients amenable to resolving the oedipal difficulties, using anxiety-provoking techniques, dealing early on with transference, stressing interpretations given the patient (in the psychoanalytic mode, of course), and basing termination on patient understanding his/her conflict (with the implication that tangible evidence is needed for this understanding). While one of these strictures would seem to apply in almost any therapy – showing evidence of change in behavior – the means to these ends is very round-about compared to behavioral methods and to various other short-term psychotherapies. In the same book edited by Budman, Gustafson[26] avers that psychoanalysis became long-term because of the emphasis on resistance, on what is called "working through," on presumed early childhood roots of problems, and on transference and dependency, and so on. Even, then, if psychoanalysis tries to be short-term, it is still burdened with the heavy conceptual aspects of depth psychology and can hardly crawl out from under this weight. It is entirely possible that short-term psychodynamic/psychoanalytic psychotherapy is neither short-term (in the more parsimonious sense of the term) nor very psychoanalytic, but is, rather, a bastard form of an attempted mixture of the two which results in no new clarity about developing a more effective psychotherapy. Too, the remaining emphasis on stringently selecting patients is not only very subjective (and thus not readily transferable to other therapists, or to training therapists) but it lacks conviction as to what is actually being done that is different from other therapies and what the outcomes are. Psychoanalytic therapists have for decades been unprepared to study and discuss outcome from psychotherapy in any meaningful ways (with a few exceptions). For example, Gustafson, in discusssing some outcome features found in the brief psychoanalytic therapies of Malan, Sifneos, and Mann, says, "Despite the radical evidence from *A Study of Brief Psychotherapy* (1963) and from Sifneos (1972) and Mann (1973), the same spectrum of opinion about brief therapy continued as before and psychoanalysis and science continued their separate ways."

Efforts, then, to retool psychoanalytic/psychodynamic psychotherapy have not proven useful scientifically or practically. While new books – and articles, and seldom are these articles *research*-oriented – continue to appear espousing the values associated with psychodynamic/psychoanalytic therapy, no substantial evidence exists for these assertions. The prospective therapist looking for better therapy methods, the to-be clinician in training and, above all, the prospective client/patient would all do well to examine short-term psychotherapies other than the "depth"-oriented ones if they are looking for more practical and more economical therapeutic experiences.

In summary of the behavioral movement it is sufficient to say that it has had the greatest impact on psychotherapy of any influence other than the Freudian one. The numbers of clinicians and experimental-minded clinicians espousing and using behavioral methods is far greater than those practicing "depth" therapies although the latter count among themselves the conceptually unresolved "eclectic" therapists. These therapists purport to draw from many theories but appear to work from a smorgasbord of ideas and techniques without knowing very well what they are doing (insofar as research support is concerned).

Behavioral therapies had their start with the most limited of populations – the handicapped – and with institutional cases, on which populations, captive as they were, many methods emanating from experimental psychology were applied to clinical, educational, and social problems. As the methodology of behavioral interventions became better established, wider ranging problems were studied and widely applied. Behavioral methods were generalized to schools, rehabilitation centers, social and educational settings, and so on. Research has been encouraging but not wholly convincing where behavioral methods are concerned. With their greater emphasis on science, on research, on outcome studies, the problems of behavioral intervention are more readily discerned and more flexible measures adopted. Behavioral intervention is far more self-correcting than any other point of view in psychotherapy or behavior change. Moreover, behavioral therapists have undertaken problems long neglected or avoided by more conventional therapists, problems related to unusual behavioral and psychological difficulties. (See Kalish's account of a debilitated infant suffering from "chronic ruminative vomiting" by behavioral methods, pp. 1-3; and Bachrach's account of how he and colleagues treated a near-death anorexic female.[27]) All this is by way of saying that the record, in its manifold ways, is far better for behavioral approaches than for psychoanalytic "depth" approaches, and probably somewhat better, especially in the more refractory cases of obsessive-compulsive, phobic and the like cases, in spite of failures and nondescript results at times, compared to other varieties of therapy. Most other varieties of therapy — see the next chapter — have not yet accumulated the research base for much of their viewpoint, the latter arising more from individual experiences with patients/clients and from speculations or very selected cases, a matter that plagues all therapy as illustrated by the above strictures on attrition.

We turn attention now to somewhat less prominent varieties of psychotherapy, although some of them are well-known enough to occasionally get some public press in magazines and newspapers.

Chapter 4

THE MAIN THEORIES OF PSYCHOTHERAPY: II. ROGERIAN, HUMANISTIC, RATIONAL-EMOTIVE THERAPIES AND BECK ON DEPRESSION

IN MY OPINION, the Rogerian movement beginning in the later 1930s, and reaching some highly visible momentum in the 1940s and 1950s, was one of the most significant movements in the history of psychotherapy.[1] The Rogerian movement helps formulate a highly convincing alternative to psychoanalytic therapy which had prevailed almost unchallenged for the previous several decades. How did Rogers do this?

Rogerian "nondirective" therapy can be characterized in several ways. As the original term, "nondirective," implies, Rogers put more stress on the role of the client in finding his/her own way in the quest for more personality integration. The therapist was not the end-all, be-all that was characterized by the Freudian outlook. In developing more self-direction through self-initiative, encouraged by the therapist in the Rogerian viewpoint, the client (note, too, that the term client, not patient, was used by Rogers) was more in charge of his/her destiny. The therapist was a "facilitator," one who understood, supported, and encouraged the client's efforts at self-examination and self-understanding. There was no great unconscious recess that had to be probed; history was incidental; and all the armamentarium of "defense" and repression and unconscious motivation was either downplayed, in the interest of client exploration of his life (as with any other exploration one might engage in), or it was ignored. In the broadest sense, however, Rogers and his students did not fully repudiate the "depth" view of human behavior; they sort of kept it in the background, and put the emphasis on the present, on the client's perception of his/her difficulties, and on the therapist's acceptance of the client's struggles for psychological freedom and independence. If the latter were the important issues, as they were for Rogerian therapy, then all the Freudian conceptual apparatus was of minor importance: What was important for the Rogerian was a kind of self-actualization (the term "self-actualization" later made cogent and popular by Maslow).[2]

Rogers and his students began to *research* psychotherapy by making (first) wire recordings (later tape recordings) of therapy sessions, and attempted to analyze the relevance of such Rogerian concepts as acceptance, unconditional regard (nonjudgemental attitudes toward the client), and empathy. These notions, mostly referring to the behavior and attitude of the therapist toward the client, showed new ways to conduct therapy and new ways to understand what was going on in therapy. These ideas also stressed the *relationships* between the client and the therapist in ways not even thought of in the Freudian mold. Therapy became more of a joint enterprise; there was no "one-upmanship" in the therapist/client interactions as there was in the Freudian viewpoint. Therapy was more "democratic," more of a sharing and one that gave increasingly more respect to the client within the course of therapy, as well as at the ending point. What was "analyzed" with Rogers was not some unconscious bulwark, but a more process-oriented exchange between client and therapist with the former leading the way and the latter put in a supportive, understanding, and reflective role. The therapist was important insofar as s/he gave the client the kind of interpersonal atmosphere in therapy that was considered productive for the client; not as a profoundly informed, silent, impersonal, holier-than-thou therapist sitting back and aloof from the client.

As one would expect, Rogers made a profound impression with his psychotherapy and research. His position challenged almost all there was to challenge in the traditional Freudian therapy. The only challenges of any consequence to Rogers came a bit later (beginning mostly in the later 1950s) with the behavioral movement, because the latter had more "science" behind what it was doing, could be applied more widely than could Rogerian therapy, and took a much broader outlook about human behavior in general with more appropriate research to back up the concepts and efforts that went into (first) behavior change and (secondly) into psychotherapy. (We have elucidated some of this point in the previous chapter.)

It has often been said in criticizing psychology that as a science, unlike physics, it does not often have "turnovers" in theory, no revolutions, no profound paradigm shifts. While that is largely true, there have been some shifts of consequence represented by both the Rogerian and the Behavioral viewpoints, although elements of both of them certainly existed to some extent before each movement became highly visible and active. One thing about psychology as science is that of a relatively greater emphasis on "practice," or on the practicality of daily life, with pure research (whatever that is) scarcely present and certainly not at all prominent (with a few exceptions); whereas physics (and astronomy) are far more "pure" in the intellectual, abstract, and scientific sense. Relative to this kind of handicap which psychology suffers from, or is embedded in, the shifts that took place in psychotherapy with the Rogerian and the Behavioral movements were significant and represent a kind of "junior shift" compared to paradigm shifts in physics and astronomy.

From the standpoint of psychology as a science and psychotherapy in particular as a field of research and study, Rogers and his students made important contributions. They were the first to truly research psychotherapy. If "self-attitudes," both positive and negative were important in describing the behavior of the client in therapy, then methods were worked out to assess "self" hypotheses from the recorded therapy sessions. If therapist "unconditional regard" and other matters were of essence, then these became research topics for the Rogerians.[3] Nothing like this had happened in the Freudian movement; they were all "above" research; they didn't have any unanswered question that they could not speculate on ad infinitum, and so on. (Some Freudian-minded psychologists, however, did begin in the 1950s and later to examine some Freudian notions, and some experimentalists — notably at Yale in the 1930s, 1940s, and 1950s — made attempts to develop experimental analogues of many Freudian concepts, but mostly from "outsiders," that is, people not in the hard core of the psychoanalytic movement.)[4]

Rogerian psychotherapy spawned a lot of other fruitful research, viz., in the direction of humanistic psychology/psychotherapy and helped give rise to psychologists with similar viewpoints to Rogers such as Maslow and Kelly. The *therapeutic* view of Rogers led to scientific research, as has been noted, and to a host of practical applications to everyday life that made sense to persons who had an intuitive grasp of what Rogers was saying without any ways and means for studying his notions. We all respond to theorists who seem to touch a sensitive cord in us, and absorb and use the ideas without testing them out scientifically; all of us cannot be scientists and none of us can be scientists all of the time. The compromise here is that Rogers showed the way to both research attacks and practical approaches to the study of psychotherapy, long overdue, which made sense and which fit far better with the rest of psychology and with the rest of "common sense" than did previous ideas. Rogers' contributions will stand prominent in the history of psychotherapy for an indefinite period of time.

HUMANISTIC PSYCHOTHERAPY

Humanistic psychotherapy is, in a way, a kind of catch-all version of Rogerian thinking.[5] The emphasis in humanistic psychotherapy and psychology is not unlike humanism in traditional historical, literary, and philosophical thought. There is greater emphasis here on the individual, on personalism (emphasizing the uniqueness of the person and the individual's perspective on self and others), and on ethical and fairness issues in human affairs. Some would say that humanistic psychotherapy is a "nonintellectual" approach to human problems (Bindrim,[6] from Corsini, p. 33).

Humanistic psychotherapy has gleaned ideas and impetus from a variety of other therapies and points of view about human existence. The "existence" part is also, as the word suggests, related to "Existential" philosophy and psychology/psychotherapy viewpoints. There exists a real mishmash in connecting existential psychotherapy with humanistic psychotherapy on the one hand and with existential philosophy on the other hand. The latter is a pessimistic view of man and existence, saying that existence (life) is evil and that human struggle is the only human good, albeit not very productive, not enough to erase the overall evil of existence. A psychotherapy which purports to help people cannot very well espouse such an existential philosophical position — in the sense of offering no hope — but such a psychotherapy can emphasize the stark realities of life and avoid a pollyanish attitude. However, this state of affairs need not concern us unduly here. Humanistic psychotherapy is very hope-oriented and positive, and its existential aspects are probably much more remote than meets the eye. In fact, Losoncy[7] (in Corsini, pp. 286-289) has a chapter entitled "Encouragement Therapy" and points out how it has drawn from existentialism, but the positive aspects here are prominent and arise, also, from one of Freud's dissenters — Alfred Adler — and from others whom Adler has influenced (Dreikurs,[8] 1968). the problems we are having in defining the humanistic movement are apparent: it, like many therapies is a fusion (or is it a conglomeration?) of many other therapies and views of mankind (or persons), and is hard to define verbally as well as operationally (that is, in terms of research, therapeutic tactics and techniques, and so forth). Humanistic psychotherapy is a general viewpoint stressing human relationships between people, stressing equity and fairness.

In order to accomplish these various goals, it is important, the humanistic psychotherapists say, to see the person's behavior as s/he sees it; from the phenomenological standpoint. This viewpoint was, of course, strongly emphasized by Rogers. Snygg and Combs[9] published a book in 1949 entitled, *Individual Behavior: A New Frame of Reference for Psychology* which espoused the phenomenological viewpoint. This publication influenced therapists, personality theorists, and others rather widely; it was later updated as *Perceptual Psychology: A Humanistic Approach to the Study of Persons* (1976); following closely on the personal/phenomenological/perceptual viewpoint that arose so clearly from Rogers' work and from others influenced by him. The Snygg and Combs later volume outlined their intention very well: ". . . both authors [i.e., [Snygg and Combs] were aware that they were outlining [in the earlier work] a new psychology, but they did not call it perceptual psychology then. They called it phenomenological psychology because it sought to understand behavior from the point of view of the behaver"[10] (p. ix). They strongly emphasized the relationship between behavior and experience, the inner and outer, so to say. The recognition, then of the importance of the inner, the personal, the phenomenological, the perceptual — find as many synonyms as you like — in contrast to *both* the Freudian (inner/historical/repressed/instinctual) and the behavioral (mainly observable behavior but all behaviorists take verbal reports, feeling states, historical facts or viewpoint into consideration) was strongly in evidence in this humanistic viewpoint.

Maslow, in his *Journals* (1982, edited by R.J. Lowry), comments on the personal viewpoint he espouses and contrasted it with Skinner's behavioral viewpoint. In the following passage, p. 242, he comments on an article by Aronoff on motivation as follows: ". . . he [e.g., [Aronoff] argues that every human being has an intrinsic inner nature, with needs, capacities, talents, temperaments, and inclinations. The human being is not an empty organism to be filled by Society." Maslow feels too much emphasis has been placed on the environment and its evil- or good-making influences on persons. While Skinner never said the organism was "empty," he did, of course, stress the environment as a set of contingencies influencing behavior. Maslow, consonant with the perceptual/phenomenological/personal/inner nature of this viewpoint, places the individual more *deliberately* in control of his being than many others do. The trouble with Maslow's position is mainly that it is an *opinion* and it is not backed up with any convincing research. It is intuitively evident that we all "see the world" through our own rose (or whatever) colored glasses, but just how much this seeing is already largely determined by the environment and by our own histories (which is to say, by order of our learning to date) is not a settled question in psychology at all. To assert that the individual perspective is so unique that it, alone, accounts for our behavior is far too exaggerated to take on a general basis. That is not to say, however, that individual preferences or ways of seeing or regarding matters are not important. However, our choices are usually related to what we've already known or experienced; wholly novel situations are not often available to us and even if they were, we would pretty well be required to go on what we already knew however similar or different it might be from the present choice.

The Maslow emphasis is not very workable for handicapped persons, for the severely neurotic (obsessive-compulsive and phobic cases, as examples), nor for psychotics. Maslow is primarily addressing the middle class, educated, somewhat culturally sophisticated person; not even the poor and indigent would come very well under his pronouncements. His psychology has grown up mainly in the Rogerian/humanistic/phenomenological/individualistic complex of factors and thus appears to apply mainly to those who would probably be a good candidate for Rogerian therapy. Maslow has not added much as far as the evidence goes to the Rogerian mold but has mainly elaborated on it and improvised, so to say, some of his own observations regarding the perceptual/individualistic point of view.

RATIONAL-EMOTIVE THERAPY

The Rational-Emotive Therapy of Albert Ellis[11] is probably the best known of the more recent therapies one would read about in current literature. However, Ellis has been around a fairly long time and has written extensively about his viewpoint. First, his method was called Rational Therapy, then later modified to include "Rational Emotive" Therapy and subsequently became known as RET. Ellis has claimed close relationship to both behavioral and cognitive behavior persuasions in psychotherapy. He has also stressed the individual viewpoint, although his counsel to clients/patients is to move away from their narrow expectations and to be more realistic about what they think of themselves and their world.

According to Ellis, people are under the assumption that life should be easier than it is, that people should love and accept them, that disappointments should not be so prominent or overwhelming in their lives, and other "irrational" beliefs. His main attack is, then, on peoples' irrational beliefs as giving rise to their problems and concerns, the reasons they consult a therapist. Ellis has listed his series of irrational beliefs that he considers prominent among his, and his colleagues' clientele. But before the irrational beliefs comes Ellis' definition:

> "It holds that when a highly charged emotional Consequence (C) follows a significant Activating Event (A), A may seem to but actually does not cause C. Instead, emotional Consequences are largely created by B — the individual's Belief System. When, therefore, an undesirable Consequence occurs, such as severe anxiety, this can usually be quickly traced to the person's irrational Beliefs, and when these Beliefs are effectively Disputed (at point D), by challenging them rationally, the disturbed Consequences disappear and eventually cease to occur" (1973, p. 167).

Ellis' main propositions, briefly stated are: 1, Man has the potential for rational and straight thinking, but this may be altered (become irrational) for a variety of reasons; 2, tendencies toward irrational thinking come from the culture, from one's childhood training and/or from current circumstances; 3, man tends to behave, think, emote, evaluate, and so on at the same time and with considerable interaction, making him a cognitive, conative, motoric (or thinking, feeling, moving, or behaving) person; 4, RET tends to be short-term inasmuch as it emphasizes cognitive, active-directive, homework-assigning and disciplinary recommendations; 5, transference in the psychoanalytic sense is not required, nor even recommended; 6, RET, like all behavioral therapies (Ellis makes his connection here explicitly with behavioral methods) uses a variety of techniques; 7, nearly all serious emotional problems stem from magical, superstitious, irrational, and unrealistic thinking; 8, ordinary psychological insight does not necessarily lead to behavior change, but focuses mainly on the definition of the problem and indicating that a problem is, indeed, present

(1973, pp. 171-173).[12] In another place Ellis says "RET is a cognitive-emotive-behavioristic method of psychotherapy which is uniquely designed to enable the individual to observe, to understand, and persistently to attack his irrational, grandiose, perfectionistic *shoulds, oughts, and musts*" (1973, p. 200).

It can be readily seen that what are loosely and largely called the person's "expectations" are contrasted with reality and create the "C" or "Consequences" that, when properly analyzed, constitute the source of the problem, that is, with the "B" or "Belief System" coming into conflict with the reality (the "Activating Event"). Ellis uses this formulation to work in a group setting, with educators and classroom teachers who wish to instruct children in more proper self-evaluation and with parents who seek to improve their and their childrens' positions vis-a-vis each other, and so on. Thus Ellis has, unlike many therapists, tried to generalize his system to other than individual therapy although the motivating conditions were individual therapy when he first started practice, research, and writing. Ellis' work has probably received more research interest than most forms of psychotherapy because it is well enough formulated to encourage specific tests of validity, areas of applicability, and relatively easy teaching to fledging therapists. It remains after thirty or so years a viable, often-studied, practical, short-term, economical, and useful psychotherapy which has wide applicability. The fact that Ellis has never been exactly clear about what he is doing in the larger conceptual sense, veering back and forth between cognitive, behavioral viewpoints, and sometimes seeming to ignore each, has seemingly not bothered Ellis nor his supporters. As all of psychotherapy gains more conceptual clarity and fully supported empirical research perhaps all psychotherapies will improve, Ellis' viewpoint being one of the foremost to gain by these improvements.

BECK'S COGNITIVE THERAPY FOR DEPRESSIVES

Beck has gained some prominence in recent years with his cognitive theory of depression.[13] His viewpoint is somewhat similar to that of Ellis, stressing the role of irrational thinking in producing depression and the so-called mood disorders. The client/patient is seen as harboring negative self-evaluations and expected outcome from his/her efforts, a kind of cyclic, "See, I told you it would not turn out right — I'm never successful!" The negativism is a kind of self-fulfilling prophesy and seems to keep the patient in a state of continuing depression and negative self-evaluation. This kind of complaining patient, Beck asserts, overgeneralizes, exaggerates complaints, alters reality to suit individual purposes, tends to see experiences as either black or white with no middle ground, and makes half-hearted efforts to change based on the already prominent notion that effort is useless since the outcome will be the same as it has always been.

While all therapists encounter clients/patients with such syndrome as Beck has described so well among depressed patients, Beck differs somewhat in how he treats these cases. Ellis on the one hand appears to select the critical cognitive issues for the client to work on – oughts, shoulds, and musts – but Beck gives more credence to the client's own selection of the cognitive states to be identified and worked on. While all therapists would likely agree that the topics and feelings and behaviors to be worked on must have salience for the client, the ways in which these efforts are capitalized on and how they are implemented in therapy appear to differ among the various cognitive therapists. Ellis has a more "older style" viewpoint and seems to leave behind the cognitive matters as espoused by the client and stress the *categorical* features of the distressing behavior under such terms as his oft-described "musts," "shoulds," and "oughts" invoked by the patient. The distressed and distressing behavior is addressed by Ellis in his already formed categories of what is wrong with people; Beck appears to let the client name the cognitive territory upon which work is to be done.

Beck stresses the importance of developing a new set of cognitions to replace the confused, self-abnegating, depressive ones used by the patient. This is done via the use of examples from life – including the patient's life – from appeals to general knowledge ("common sense" information about what is good or bad for one), from recognizing what is healthful and not healthful in one's behavior, feelings and cognitions (attitudes), and by utilizing the patient's own suggestions based on other facets of one's life that seem to go fairly well. "You do well in this area of your life, why, then, do you do so poorly in this correspondingly similar area of your life? – What's the difference?" might be the therapist's message to the client.

This emphasis on cognitions as the entering point in treating the patient's distress, and as the main basis of therapeutic exchange between patient and therapist, raises a most interesting point about *cognitive* behavior therapy. We have already seen that Ellis gives homework assignments and is, himself, an active, participating member of the therapeutic team. While Beck does not eschew behavioral efforts – he sometimes appears to regard analogue situations, *in vivo* experiences and imaginal performance along with cognitive expressiveness – he does not stress them as much as does Ellis. If the emphasis is truly on cognitive matters, then with successful change in this aspect of one's being, the behavioral "fall out" should be positive: Change the inside and the outside will follow. Of course, this is the original Freudian notion, except for the fact that Freud stressed the highly refractory-to-change aspects of the inner life, the depth/suppression/defensive nature of this life, and so on, far more than contemporary cognitive therapists. However, the cognitive therapists like Beck seem to draw more on the traditional depth model in the way they write, think, and act vis-a-vis the patients' cognitive reporting. This issue – how much "cognitive" is enough and how much too much – is a very real problem and one that all therapists, regardless of other aspects of their theory and practice, divide themselves. Cognitions blend into behavior and behavior blends into cognitions; where the lines are drawn in a practical sense may depend more upon the idiosyncracies of the therapist and the patient than upon any scientific matters, and may, also, differ greatly between therapists of ostensibly the same persuasion at different times and with different clients. One of the issues that raises cognitive theories-therapies to such prominence, whether they are cognitive alone or cognitive/behavioral, is that the therapist must be sensitive to what the client/patient reports, as verbal (or other) behavior, and the labels should not get in the way of clarification, understanding, or other considerations. Perhaps if more emphasis were put on what the patient actually does and says, and less on the categorical assignments of these activities, we would gain more understanding of how to help people and would foment fewer squabbles about the "meaning" of what's what with the client. Apropos of the statement that cognitive and behavioral matters are interlaced (to accede momentarily to this unfortunate dichotomy), Bandura[14] (1977) has indicated from his research findings that direct behavioral intervention enhances the self-efficacy results for the patient, compared to only cognitive clarification: It is another way of saying one cannot have behavior without cognitions and vice versa. The more strict behaviors have not denied that cognitions "exist" but that they are not the most fortunate and useful of concepts in trying to understand change and control behavior. The most practical way out of this unfortunate impasse, this unneeded dichotomy between cognitions and behavior, is to take the problem where it is and try to form change principles that will be effective. All else is secondary, or even unnecessary.

The emphasis then on cognitions as if they were a separate and distinct matter, as if they were the "key" to psychotherapy and behavior change, cannot be other than misleading, scientifically and practically. If what the client conveys to us as therapists, by mood, emotional display, words, reports on dreams, or whatnot, we have no choice at first other than to take these revelations at face value; how they relate to subsequent change efforts is often very complex and obliges us as therapists to be flexible in how we proceed and how we talk about and evaluate what we do. Just assigning this or that interaction to "cognitive" categories, holding these up in turn as the end-all/be-all of what is important with the client, is not only not true, it is not at all advisable or parsimonious.

However, all these scientific, conceptual, and semantic issues aside, what the reader of this book, as client, or as therapist gets from this discussion should be a high respect for caution. The client will simply want to find and relate to a good and effective therapist — irrespective of his/her "theory" — and what the therapist will want is a client who can respond to his/her therapeutic leadership; all of this is irrespective of whether we call this or that exchange in therapy "cognitive" or "behavioral." Of course, I am biased in favor of the behavioral viewpoint, because as has been said, the bottom line is always: Did the behavior change? Understanding how the client feels, emotes, behaves, views, etc. his/her behavior (his/her reasons for coming to therapy) is all to be taken into consideration – how else could one get started in therapy with self-reporting adults? – but the assignment of conceptual categories to the patient's behavior should not interfere with the process of communication or the process of change. After we get more expert at both of these matters – early or initial communication and the longer process of change – we can become more expert in dividing up the complex issues and assigning predictive relevance to this or that behavior. We are certainly not at this enviable position now, and there is little promise we are making very great strides; psychotherapy will probably stumble along for some time before it reaches a truly scientific, practical, and economical position.

OTHER COGNITIVE POSITIONS

The cognitive movement within and without behavioral therapy has been in evidence for several years. Cognitive emphases and the recognition of cognitive aspects of human functioning have, of couse, been with us since man began to think about himself. Meichenbaum[15] (1977), indeed, emphasized the "thinking" aspects in his therapy and called it *Cognitive Behavior Modification.* He says, "As will become evident . . . such a description exemplifies the cognitive-behavior modification approach – an analysis of the thinking processes involved in performing a task, rather than merely the assessment of the product or outcome of the performance" (p. 13). And ". . . inner speech is one aspect of the thinking process . . ." (p. 13). It is clear, then, that the cognitive psychologists and psychotherapists who, over the past decade or so have emphasized this position have gone "inside" the organism, as it were, and sought clues as to why people behaved overtly as they did. The emphasis has been on covert processes, not on overt ones.

Foreyt and Goodrick[16] (1981, in Corsini, p. 133) state that cognitive processes affect behavior, and that such processes can be changed by their own kind (i.e., cognitive processes) as well as behavioral processes. These authors further note that cognitive therapy is different from traditional depth therapy in that the cognitive process targeted for change are in the here and now (even in the therapist's office, or in their assignments carried home with them), and not seen as the accumulated influence from the past now provoking the present difficulties. Foreyt and Goodrick also note the long history of cognitive therapists, including from Korzybski, Johnson, Kelley, Phillips, Frank, early Ellis, and so on, and going back 75 years or longer. The recent emphasis, then, on cognitive therapy has been somewhat a matter of old wine in new bottles, and perhaps not the innovation it has purported to be. This is particularly the case when we stop to consider that today's research techniques are considerably advanced over what they were 6 to 8 decades ago and should therefore mirror some important advances in reference to cognitive matters. In other branches of psychology, cognitive influences seem to have been more substantial (in social psychology) than in clinical and psychotherapy areas.

It is not so much that cognitive psychotherapists are lacking in realization that advances should be more noticeable, it is that the hard work of research has simply not been done to advance the cause of cognitive therapy. Mahoney (1977) ably states what cognitive intervention should or might do: better and more reliable methods of cognitive assessment; how cognition influences behavior; how cognitive states remain fluid or constant; relating cognitive matters directly to psychotherapy; and continuing reappraisal of how cognitions figure saliently in psychotherapy (p. 10, paraphrased points).

As has been evident in several places in this book, the criticisms of behavioral techniques rests mainly on their being somewhat superficial, external to the person being treated (or studied) and the techniques, as stated, appear to have been inconsistent in their results. Many would say behaviorists have extrapolated too easily and too much from animal studies to the human situation, the latter being under control of the way the person sees things (his/her perceptions). All of this may not be as planned by the researcher, the therapist or anyone else other than the person under consideration. In other words, the limits of behavioral techniques has been laid bare more saliently in psychotherapy than in any other domain, probably because of the complexity of the therapy situation and because of the nature of the interactional setting of the therapist and the client (Foreyt and Goodrick, 1981, p. 135). Cognitive therapy was born, it would seem, out of realization that the behavioral formulations did not pan out as expected.

Some of the remedies for the strict behavioral approach are seen in the following instances of therapeutic techniques: Cognitive self-instruction, based on how the client sees his/her problems and what changes are called for by what methods; covert modeling or subjective rehearsal of target behaviors, especially in stressful situations; coping skills training through imaginative processes; self-application of stress management in anxiety situations; stress inoculation based on better assessment of the stress provoking situations; improving means-ends understanding of how the individual can, for himself, improve problem solving; and viewing personal problems as essentially scientific problems in the way they are stated, analyzed, and worked on. These are all ways of handing over to the client the skills of the therapist (as an "outsider") and building them into the repertoires of the client, first under the instructions of the therapy, then under the person's own control.

It takes no acumen to see, however, that these cognitive measures are really extensions of what have already been practiced behaviorally for decades. Whatever differences they portray seem to hinge on the assumption that only the client's perspective is valid. However, much we may argue that all treatment must emanate from the client's complaints, that does not mean that whatever perspective the client has it is perforce better than that of the therapist. It may be; but not necessarily so, and it is not a great error to assume that the therapist can and does know something that will be effective for the client or that the client's interests are necessarily abdicated when the therapist makes moves from his/her vantage point. The subtleties of engaging the client effective in his/her own remedial processes is a very delicate matter — in some cases, but not all — and does not hinge on either the therapist or the client being "right." However one may argue about the client's role in self-help, all therapists, if their hearts are in the right place, want to be of use to the client; the role of each is not an all-or-none matter. Clinicians and especially psychotherapists are still reeling from the impact of the Freudian model of client helplessness and dependence, and fail to break down the problem of client involvement at the outset, or later on as well, in proper proportion to what the client wants, needs, and can use. As the quote above from Bandura indicates, the cognitive measures have to have some behavioral payoff for sake of judging efficacy, and if the client can translate the cognitive (instructional) matters into behavior, that is what we want. Even if the client says only, "I feel better but I don't act any differently," it is still important to know that (for both client and therapist) but also important to know that the client has to have had some interactions with his/her world to discern "feeling better." It was found in one study over a two-year period that university students with a mean age of 23 years, reported on a 22-item follow-up questionnaire (after therapy) that behavior change was judged to come more reliable, sooner and to contribute better to progress than feeling change.[17] Therapists, consonant with their more traditional training — more traditional than this book espouses — were surprised at this finding; when therapists themselves were asked to reply to the same follow-up questionnaire (under the instructions, "answer these questions as you think an average successful client would answer them"), they tended to rate feelings uppermost. Client and therapist orientations are lacking concordance in some important ways; to assume that the client's viewpoint can be clearly envisioned and made the basis of therapy in the total sense espoused by the cognitive therapists is certainly contrary to a lot of evidence we have concerning client and therapist's similarities in how they view therapy, its process, and its outcomes. Discerning the client's innermost being is most unlikely, by both therapist and client.

Foreyt and Goodrick indicate that many of the cognitive "states" (or whatever they are to be called) are nonspecific[18] (1981, p. 142). Whether cognitive efforts actually do bring the mentalistic or subjective factors into bolder relief and into specific domains is a moot point. It is well known that many nonspecific factors help account for all kinds of change in psychotherapy — or, better, that specific factors do not yield up as much explanation of therapy change as one would like — so it is highly unlikely that cognitive factors, usually unspecific as they inherently are and as subjective as they are (until tested out via behavior change) can provide the specifics needed for change, especially in refractory cases such as severe obsessive-compulsive and phobic problem areas. The cognitive movement might be convincing to some if it were really as advanced and important as some say; but there is simply no evidence that this is true, and the sooner and the better we realize it, the more we are likely to advanced across all fronts in the study and delivery of psychotherapy.

Another important question along these same lines is why we tend, intuitively perhaps, to regard our subjective states as so central to our being. When we have a toothache, it is not uncommon that we are unable to tell exactly which tooth is the problem. The dentist can tell a lot more. Countless other examples of the same phenomenon in trying to locate the source of pains or discomfort in our head region, in our back, and so forth. The nervous system is not constructed in a way that gives us easy access to the exact location of discomfort; a general area sensitivity seems to be about all we can muster with accuracy. People are equally often incapable of telling exactly how they feel about some experience knowing only that they have a generalized "good" or "bad" feeling (they might say "perception"), and let it go at that. From an evolutionary standpoint, the organism needs to know only enough to flee or to fight; discomfort is a generalized state, as is fear, foreboding, apprehension, and the like, and is not required, so to speak, by nature, to be highly specific in labeling the source of psychological difficulty or stress or even pain. All kinds of distress may be regarded as unconditional stimuli, in the Pavlovian model, which get conditioned to particular situations that then tell the organism where lies the difficulty in an environmental sense. Now comes the cognitive therapists to say that the innermost has been too long neglected and there is where we will hit "pay dirt." Thus far there has been little evidence to support these claims.

A further point along this same line: A number of years ago the "projective testing" movement got under way, mostly based on the American use of the Rorschach Ink Blot cards. There was a great movement toward the inner searching of persons using the Rorschach, the TAT (Thematic Apperception Test) and other projective techniques. Most of these, save for the Rorschach, have now died out and little is heard from their usefulness. While no one piece of research dismissed the projective devices out-of-hand, the gradual realization that they did not produce much, took lots of time that could be spent in more gainful activities with the patient, and tended to be unreliable as well all agreed (their lack of validity showed they did not predict well). In the meanwhile the more objective and standardizable personality, temperament, and interest questionnaires are flourishing where tests are used and, moreover, fit well into the hands of computers that can give printouts of results, as well as reports of a "profile" nature, with speed and accuracy (accuracy in relation to the internal features of the inventory or questionnaire itself).

The cognitive behavioral movement will, then, have to gain a lot more ground if it is to be a viable way to understand people, to assess human characteristics, to provide therapy and to contribute to the study of behavior change outcome. The coupling of cognitive factors with behavioral ones — as implied in the "cognitive-behavioral terminology — is primarily a statement about where to look for *some* clues as to how and why people behave as they do, but the instruction that must come to all of psychology, whatever the theoretical viewpoint, is whether the behavior changes as a result of the knowledge received by any process whatsoever.

Chapter 5

THE NEWER PSYCHOTHERAPIES, AUXILIARY THERAPIES AND JAPANESE THERAPY

IN THE PAST twenty years or so there has been a considerable proliferation of "new" psychotherapies (Herink, 1980; Corsini, 1973, 1981; Patterson, 1974; Rosenbaum, 1984).[1] The more "standard" psychotherapies that have been around a considerable length of time (Corsini, 1974, 1981; Patterson, 1974) have been based on behavioral or learning theory models, on psychoanalytic/psychodynamic viewpoints, and on blends of these two. Now comes a group of "new" therapies which seem not to have as strong anchorage points as the more established therapies, and have, of course, not had time to build a solid research base for their views and activities.

A brief but cogent review of the newer psychotherapies is found in the book by Harper (1975) bearing the same name: *The New Psychotherapies.*[2] This book lists several psychotherapies that are more outgrowths of already evident trends – e.g., Reality Therapy by William Glasser; Operant Conditioning which is not a therapy per se but a number of applications of Skinnerian conditioning work and has been around too long to be called new; Aversion Therapy which also is an outgrowth of both Pavlovian and Skinnerian studies; and Morita therapy which has been in existence in Japan since about 1920. Some of these therapies appear new because they have not been fully recognized before, and some like Morita therapy have had their currency elsewhere.

The newer therapies group themselves in several ways: Those based on learning (behavioral) principles such as conditioning therapies, aversion therapy, Implosion Therapy; those following a more "depth" oriented view such as the "body therapies" of Reich (Orgone therapy or revetotherapy); Lowen ("Bio-Energetics," an offshoot of Reichian therapy); Janov ("Primal Therapy"); and Luthe ("Autogenic Therapy"); and miscellaneous other therapies with varied backgrounds and viewpoints.[3]

Other than to state that some of these are among the newer therapies on the scene, and to note that they contribute quite sparingly to their own research support (perhaps Janov, Luthe, & Stampfl have the best research support), it can be said that they locate much of the problem of the individual in the body, in its "armour," its rigidity, in its kind of ossification of early on emotional neglect, trauma, and conflict. Just talking about problems, some of these therapists say, is not enough; one must get to the body rigidification which exemplifies, "solidifies" and supports the psychological damage already done. The incrustations, so to say, have to be attacked therapeutically and not just with the verbal, emotional, and social consequences of the distress. Harper has pointed out that these body therapies do not emphasize the client's consciousness regarding "defense" as important in maintaining the disturbance. The body armour has been "attacked" therapeutically in the sense of an aggressive assault on the person's emotional difficulties; the therapy matter is largely in the therapist's hands once some preliminary data about the patient are obtained. In some respects, then, they are depth-oriented and in some ways learning-based; the corrective efforts are learning-based, but the theory of origin are depth-related. Other varieties of these body-oriented therapies have also surfaced, e.g., Rolfing originated by Ida Rolf, a therapy based on very vigorous body contacts; Postural integration based on deep-tissue-physical manipulations; Soma therapy; and so on (see Corsini, 1981, pp. 97-106 for more complete descriptions).[4] It is highly likely that most of these newer therapies are short-term although they do not espouse such a position; that they are more behavioral than their originators often admit or realize; that they combine at the theoretical level various selections from psychodynamic theory, ending up straddling behavioral and depth notions; and tend to be very weak in the cognitive areas. Many of these newer therapies, so-called, have been current or even existed prior to much of the recent cognitive movement, hence have not been influenced by the latter.

The newer therapies of the "body" type have been applied to a more select group of clients/patients than most outpatient "talking" therapies, reserving such procedures as primal scream, bioenergetic and autogenic therapy to seemingly more formidable cases, to problems appearing to require specialized techniques, and, of course, to patients/clients selecting, or readily submitting, to these therapies. To some extent similar remarks may apply to the aversion therapy offshoot from behavioral therapy. Very little is now known about how patients select certain therapies, or therapists, other than through ordinary referral means; a bit more is known about how therapists select patients, especially for psychoanalysis; in all, the process of matching therapist, technique, and patient is not a ready or clear matter. Judgements and evaluations of who gets what therapy for how long and under what circumstances, remains almost entirely in the exclusive realm of not well-planned and very occasional research studies. The overall problem of the variety of therapies being evenly distributed to the variety of clients seeking help over a wide range of problems is virtually nonexistent. Claim then of therapeutic success with given types of patients/clients with rare exceptions is not a very meaningful generalization. One has to fly by the seat of his pants and go on the impressions one has from reading about a therapy (or therapist); or taking the recommendations of present or former clients/patients who seem to know first-hand a bit more than anyone else, and at this time more than the research literature can supply.

AUXILIARY THERAPIES

The term "auxiliary therapies" may appear a bit invidious and slighting to some. What is usually meant by this term is therapy that is not in the mainstream of therapeutic activity; but is regarded as supportive, adjunctive, supplemental, diversionary, or the like (Brown, McDowell, and Smith, 1981).[5] In contributing to this area of therapy, I referred to "supportive" therapies in the same book.

Auxiliary therapies include among others, writing therapy, dance therapy, poetry therapy, art therapy, music therapy, bibliotherapy, drama, and, most recently, the use of the computer. Any of these supportive or auxiliary therapies can be used alone, in combinations with each other, and/or in conjunction with standard verbal therapies of any sort. Hospitals have been the first and foremost to use bibliotherapy; poetry therapy has been used with the elderly; dance and music therapy with the handicapped; and the computer has been used — and will be increasingly used — with the usual client or patient, especially in university counseling centers and mental health units (often on an experimental basis).

While these supplemental or supportive therapies gain their names from the *activities* they employ (music, dance, poetry, etc.) they are often related to more conventional therapies, most often psychoanalytic/psychodynamic therapies. Sometimes these therapies are also called *expressive* therapies, emphasizing their role in encouraging emotional expressiveness by the participants, when face to face "talking therapies" appear not to work as well, or when they are *chosen* by clients who are somewhat reticent verbally and yet have emotional matters to express somehow.

In trying to summarize the role of these supportive therapies, I elsewhere (Brown, McDowell & Smith, 1981, pp. 396-397) stated that they were relatively new in applications, had select areas of application, had typically played a secondary role to other therapies, can often be combined well with talking by the client (that is, are not exclusively art, poetry, etc.), are primarily therapies of emotional release (not so much problem solving), show scattered and inconsistent results in follow-up studies (which are scarce), lack research sophistication in their respective literatures, and have not commanded the respect they merit among general therapists of all persuasions.[6] In short, these supportive or auxiliary therapies are kind of a "mixed bag" insofar as the full range of professional support for them is concerned (training, research, application, integration into clinical settings, etc.); but in spite of all these lacks they appear promising and should certainly be made available on a wider basis to clients than is now the case. The sharing, social communication, expressiveness, and emotional release found in various use of these therapies, especially among handicapped populations, is worth far more employment and study than they have gotten. The promise is greater than their present position indicates; but the professionals following these therapies must look to far greater substance in the way of research, training, and institutional usage.

While the expressive/supportive/auxiliary therapies tend to be colored by psychoanalytic notions, they are just as behavioral as any other therapy, and can be conceptualized in behavioral terms more appropriately if my study of their procedures and usefulness is correct (Phillips, 1984).[7]

One difficulty with the supportive therapies is that the practitioners are not well-trained in psychology or psychotherapy. They often think all that one has to do is give a client a piece of paper, a pencil (or crayon or paints), a musical instrument, etc., and let them express their innermost being. The role of instructions, verbal interactions with the client, what (in art therapy, for example) color and form and use of space mean — if, indeed, they mean anything in particular — are all bulwarks behind which art therapists reside rather than studying these allegedly important considerations and arriving at some useful procedures, theories, and training modules. As and when the expressive, supportive, auxiliary therapies mature, they will have to concentrate more on the overall psychological aspects of what they are doing, rather than simply regarding "movement," "painting," "singing" (or other musical expression), "writing," etc. as the important ingredient. It may matter little or naught what the client actually *does* (paint, draw, move, play music, etc.) and much more on what the setting calls for and how the therapist interacts with the patient; the medium is *not* the message, the setting is the message!

The more the expressive, supportive, and auxiliary therapists tout their wares, the more it will be incumbent upon them to do the proper research to better identify what they say (and do), or show how improvements on their basic premises might be achieved. Their promise appears to be greatest in the area of social communication matrices, not in the particulars of the expressive art itself; but only time and definitive research will tell us which way is the more productive, emphasizing the content or the setting.

Psychotherapy by Computer

Is it really possible to conduct what is loosely called psychotherapy by computer? It evidently is if we are to take present trends seriously. A computer acts as a therapist by being programmed to raise questions, to branch out from these questions, and to offer various kinds of suggestions, interpretations, solutions, etc., similar to what a real live therapist would do. But how can the computer keep up with the patient? How can the computer synthesize what the client says? How can the computer take what the client says and project possible additional questions or suggestions which follow up on the lead the client starts? In short, how can a computer judge what to do and be appropriate in responding to the client?

Computers have been used for some time in regard to health survey or habits. I distinctly remember answering about a 250-items set of questions on my health habits, feelings, complaints, etc. several years ago when I underwent a general physical examination. I had no trouble with the questions or the responses provided me by the computer terminal on which I was recording the answers. It was much like typing in one respect; it was like answering questions posed by a physician or physician's assistant. It was interesting! But that is different from delving into personal problems; after all, a list of health habits is not a personality profile, it is not psychotherapy. True. But if you look at protocols that are derived from psychotherapy from almost any vantage point, you will see a strong resemblance to a question-and-answer framework. I have done what I call "Writing Therapy" for over 20 years.[8] It is a format not unlike what the computer does. In writing therapy, the client comes in for an appointment and sits down with a notebook to write about his/her concerns. Instructions tell the client to write as candidly as possible for 50 minutes (just as if s/he were in a regular therapy hour), and to return the next week at the same time; it is important to keep an appointment and writing time structure so that, as with regular therapy, the client brings his/her concerns forward at the appointed time. Scheduling of appointments, however, is much easier with writing therapy since the client is not seen at the time of the writing therapy appointment — and is usually not seen until the writing series is completed — and the therapist has freedom to respond to what the client has written at any point in time before the client returns for the next writing session.

After the client has written his/her concerns, the writing notebook is turned into the secretary for safe keeping in a locked file. The therapist takes out the protocol and "answers" it. This reply usually takes about 15 minutes with most writing therapy protocols; the client being able in 50 minutes to write only about 3 to 5 pages. The therapist replies by numbering the main points the client has stated in the left margin of the paper, and may underline key words, phrases, or even sentences. An example of a writing therapy protocol follows:

EXAMPLE OF WRITING THERAPY PROTOCOL

Therapist
Notes

"This is my first writing and I hardly know how to be-
gin. I imagine I am talking to you in person — Mr. or
1 Mrs. Therapist. I know not which, but that may not be
important — and so I will go on that basis.
2 My main problem, I think, is that I lose my temper too
readily.
Just this morning I blew up at my roommate because he
didn't put his dirty clothes in the hamper before he
went off to class and to work. "Why should I have to
pick up after you?" I said.
3 He just smiled and walked out — very exasperating be-
4 havior to me. He also does not bring in milk and bread
and jelly and things like that for our snack, which we
keep in our small refrigerator . . . but he's always there
to eat my offerings. I get so so angry with him I just
5 about blow up. Well, uh, you could say I do blow up
now and then.
6 He also will pick up his mail at the desk downstairs and
not bring up mine but I always bring up his mail. He
never even thanks me for it if he sees me come in with it
after class or work. He is really a rude, and inconsider-
ate person, and I am just beside myself not knowing
7 what to do about him and this situation. At other times
8 he can be agreeable . . . like when we're going out for a
movie or to a dance . . . or even if we are just quietly
studying at night. He may even be friendly at those
times and you'd never know he was such a selfish per-
son if you saw him on these better occasions.

Therapist's Reply to Client Writing Therapy

"Thank you for giving a clear and succinct account of your concerns with your roommate. The left margin of your paper has some numbering, and some words or phrases are underlined, drawing attention to what you have said which will be replied to in this writing by your therapist. You have said that it makes no difference if I am a "Mr." or "Mrs." therapist and that is right. What does matter is how you cope with the things you have experienced as frustration: Nos. 2-8, each being a bit different but all subsumable under one general topic "frustration" with your roommate. Also, by implication, you have shown how you give in to your roommate, albeit in exasperation, but nonetheless yielding to him. All this leads to your problem: blowing up. It is understandable that you blow up. What needs changing is not the blowing up, per se, but recasting the conditions that lead to so much repeated exasperation and the eventual blowing up. It might be useful to think about talking with your roommate when you are not being provoked, sometime when you're in a good mood with each other, and try to set down, perhaps in writing, how you and he can divide up duties, do each others favors, and the like; and see how he responds. If you approach him only critically, when you are thorougly exasperated, he then fights back with indifference, a smirk, or just walking out on you. He is escaping your concerns; you need to approach him when the atmosphere is better. Let us work on this approach. See you next time . . ."

Some explanations are indicated in responding to the client's writing therapy protocol. First, this is only one of four pages the client wrote; he gave some other examples of losing his temper with his parents during phone calls, usually concerning money, his studying and grades, and his going out on dates. He would become "exasperated," as he so frequently put it, with parental admonitions to him. He also told of one interaction with a professor concerning a paper he had written in which he got a "B" — but felt he deserved an "A." The professor admonished him — "frustrating" the client — by pointing up some pretty obvious flaws in his paper. And so on . . .

The client, then, presented two sets of conditions in this very first writing, that caused him problems — being taken advantage of by his roommate (we may later hear more about this issue and about others his own age who seem to him to take advantage of him), and his being subject to remonstrations by parents and even the professor about his conduct, broadly speaking, all leading to "exasperation" and temper outbursts (although occasionally he "holds his temper" as with the professor, since blowing up might make matters worse, he averred).

Well, here we have the essence of an interaction between client and therapist. I submit that this interaction is, in structure and in principle, about like any one would encounter if one eavesdropped on a private therapist/client discussion, heard a tape recording of a therapy session, or read other writing therapy protocols.

Even though most therapy interactions, as posited here, are very similar, there are many ways in which one can look at the therapy session and many things one can identify as "problem areas." It is a kind of "fielder's choice" for therapists — perhaps that is why there are so many so-called types of therapy.

The Writing Therapy example is given to show several things: How fundamentally simple and straightforward most therapy interactions are (provided, of course, that the client is self-disclosing, which this young man certainly was). If it is this fundamentally straightforward, why can it not be put on a computer with appropriate interspersed replies by the therapist — "I see what you're saying . . . please go on" and the like. Or, after the client has revealed a number of instances of his/her problems, the computer could, under proper instructions, say something like: "I see all these examples are pretty much alike — e.g., you *let* someone take advantage of you by not speaking up sooner — is that not correct?" and the like. The computer can also be programmed to give suggestions: "Several suggestions for dealing with your frustration might include: speak up earlier to your roommate when things are not in bad shape, when you're feeling o.k. about each other . . . write out a list of things *you* can do and what you suggest *he* might do to keep the routine going well . . . and ask for a general review of your relationship some time in a day or two so you both can think about it clearly and be ready for an objective review of matters." And so forth.

Very often people know what to do to remedy their problems, they just need help in asserting this knowledge and timing it correctly. Your approval — Mr./Mrs. Therapist — or Mr./Mrs. Computer — may be just the added incentive, a little "push" that gets the matter of correction under way. With this push, you can then go forth on your own.

In Writing Therapy the therapist also breaks down the problem presentation into smaller, more manageable units. You cannot correct everything at once; it must be taken step-by-step, a little bit at a time . . . what the behavior therapist calls "successive approximations" to a goal or objective. We intuitively work that way, anyhow, when we solve problems that come easier for us; the ones that are harder for us to solve we try to do all-at-once, and simply get more frustrated as a result, because most problems, especially if emotionally reacted to, and if fairly chronic in our lives, are not solved that summarily. They take time! The computer can be programmed to do the same things, say the same things, that the writing therapist does, or that, even the regular therapist does in his/her office!

Also, the computer therapist, if we can call it that, can be programmed to react not only to a whole protocol, such as in the Writing Therapy case above, but can be programmed to react to given segments of the therapist's protocol. For example, suppose the client comes for help owing to not being able to concentrate, therefore not getting work done on time on the job or in school; this, in turn, leads to our familiar state — "frustration" — and ramifies into other emotional directions resulting in depression, worry, self-recrimination, anger at the provoking situations (roommate, parents, professor, other friends, etc.); and so we end up with a big dark cloud over our client's life. The computer can take the "poor concentration" label and set up some procedures for remedying it, which the client will then practice at home and bring back the results to the computer. The computer might say:

C.: You don't concentrate well because you do not go about the job correctly. Let us try this:

a) arrange a time/place for studying, keep it inviolate;
b) read one — just one — paragraph, stop and say back to yourself what you've read; don't go on until you can do that satisfactorily;

c) take your time; read slowly at first; hold yourself to the *task* of remembering, not how fast you can go;
d) after a small section of a chapter, or perhaps even just a few paragraphs, stop and recite again, and so on;
e) don't let this slowed-down procedure bother you; if you had a sprained ankle you would not expect immediately to run the 100-yard dash, you'd need time to recover; you're in a "recovery" period in regard to concentrating.

and so forth . . .

Problems have logical, understandable, causal conditions that bring them about; they also have logical properties that lead to correction. Much of therapy, or counseling, or remedial instruction, or what-not, consist in breaking down a problem to more manageable size, and proceeding with corrections. The strain comes from having to slow down, to change one's tactics, not with the enormity of the problem. Traditional therapies have called "the problem" an enormity; that is simply not true; the enormity, if one wants to note this fact, comes from not having good remedial measures at hand and from not practicing them forthwith. Most therapy can work well in a short time . . . long, long periods are not needed. The results from Writing Therapy, as well as from outpatient mental health clinic results — which we have noted in earlier chapters — and from upcoming computer help — will testify to the importance of solutions, workable measures that can be put into force to correct, or noticeably ameliorate, problems.

What has computer therapy done? How has it helped?

Schwartz[9] is a good compendium on the use of computers in various mental health areas, including psychotherapy. The reference is mostly not a research-oriented one, but it does give overview of dozens of uses of computers in these areas that will be of value to the therapist, particularly, and to the patient as well. It is important to realize that a computer can do only what people prepare (program) it to do; this goes for test construction, medical or mental health interviewing, and so forth. Standards already exist for these matters and the computer usages have to bow to these standards. For example, the American Psychological Association has published standards for test construction and use.[10] In the field of actual programs dealing with psychotherapy, however, progress equal to the standardized test criteria have not been reached so one would have to use programmed psychotherapy with caution.

Possibly the first and best use of the computer in psychotherapy is a supplemental and adjunct one; the computer can extend and enhance the therapist's role in several respects: First, by helping the client organize thinking and feeling (similar to the Writing Therapy excerpt above); second, by presenting simulation "games" or interactions which might typify the client's reactions to others; third, by assisting the client in developing better problem-solving or frustration tolerance; and fourth, by increasing longer-term planning procedures. These are all matched, incidentally, in the Writing Therapy brief presented above. The computer may be doing more expeditiously what the therapist in person, or via Writing Therapy is doing; if so, this can be a great help in therapy of the ordinary face-to-face kind (Schwartz, 1984, pp. 319-320).

As to preparation for therapy, general psychological/psychiatric assessment may be performed well by the computer, and much more expeditiously than can a person. Schwartz (1984, pp. 205-207) reviews some results from 683 patients from a variety of settings responding to a computer with a program covering 29 different "life areas" (e.g., job, family, sex, sleep, use of alcohol, etc.)[11] The computer survey was able to cover twice as many areas as the human interviewer; it was able to identify more specific problem areas of salience to people; it printed out a composite problem-oriented list of items for subsequent therapeutic examination or other consideration. Altogether the computer had a better summary (or overview), better coverage of areas and of items within areas, and more incisive information on particular areas of potential use in therapy. These findings suggest how the computer could be used at the intake interview and how the resulting information could be used to launch therapy. Whether all this comprehensiveness is needed is, of course, another problem; only research over time will tell if it is important to have the wide coverage, or whether any reasonably salient introduction point (as in the Writing Therapy protocol, above) is sufficient to get the patient or client into the therapeutic interaction.

An example of a computer in operation is "Eliza," named after Eliza Doolittle in G.B. Shaw's play, *Pygmalion.* Eliza is programmed to reply to certain key words in what the person (client) typed in, not unlike the underlined or number word or phrase found in the Writing Therapy example. Questions are then asked about this key word, intended to draw out and fill in the thinking or feeling behind the use of the key word. The computer goes on to other key words, and so on.

What is not now clear about computers in therapeutic use is whether they produce as good as or better results, according to some set of criteria used with regular therapy. In time we will be able to answer these questions more ably; for now, the computer can help the therapist in the ways suggested and can highlight what kinds of information and interactions are possible; it provides an interactional structure against which to compare actual therapy for purposes of salience, economy, and comprehensiveness; even aside from the taking-the-place-of-the-therapist, which is certainly not now possible.

Getting somewhat into the content of therapy via existing theories, computers have been programmed to operate from the standpoint of Rational-Emotive Therapy, Gestalt Therapy, Transactional Analysis, and Neuro-Linguistic Programming (NLP), suggesting how the therapies that are more specific in content and procedure can be the basis of simulation. We have already seen that all therapies appear to be subject to the same attrition curve;

now it is possible that they may all be reduced, with the help of the computer, to basic *strategies, questions, and outcomes*. That would be a remarkable achievement if it could be brought about, and it looks as if it would be feasible – in time, and given the proper research – because the similarities among therapies, especially "talking" ones, are striking, as are results. Such a set of similarities would then prove to be a good baseline for detecting and analyzing differences that might be important in how well people respond to therapy, who needs more treatment and for what reasons, and so forth.

JAPANESE THERAPIES

Of all the new trends in psychotherapy, perhaps the most neglected and misunderstood are the Japanese therapies.[12] They have been around a long time – Morita therapy, for example, since the 1920's – but the Japanese therapies have not penetrated the American scene until recently, thanks mostly to the efforts of Reynolds (1976, 1980, 1983). Morita and Naikan therapy are both well-known and practiced in Japan, Morita therapy for over six decades. The importance of Morita therapy in Japan – as well as all forms of psychotherapy practiced in Japan – suggest we take them more seriously. The exchange of ideas alone should be worth a great deal; the content and practice of Japanese therapies may be instructive to Westerners in general and to the American psychotherapy membership in particular.

Morita Therapy

Morita therapy was formulated in the 1920s by one, Morita Shoma, a philosopher-psychiatrist steeped in Buddhist thought, but with his ideas tempered by interactions with his patients. Most therapies have begun in this manner, that is, from some broad theoretical base fused with current experiences with clients or patients. Reynolds (1980, pp. 4-5) suggests Morita therapy is best suited to persons with mild but persistent and somewhat debilitating interpersonal distress. The diagnostic title here is *shinkeishitsu* neuroses.[13] Compared to the widespread use of therapies in the USA – alas! there are hundreds of them – Morita therapy had, as of the mid-to-late 1970s, less than 100 therapists scattered among several dozen hospitals and mental health groups in all of Japan. Reynolds says, ". . . it is sufficient to point out that the majority of patients treated are young (in their twenties and thirties) and self-conscious (p. 6)," a description remarkably similar to many outpatient populations in the USA, and particularly similar to the clientele found in college and university counseling centers.

The typical Morita therapy client is self-conscious and lacks self-confidence. This client may be treated on an outpatient basis, or in a hospital, typically for a week. The term "hospital" is somewhat misleading; it is more a retreat or rest time during which the client/patient is kept in almost total isolation, served food but without any entertainment or diversions, and is visited daily by his/her therapist. Therapists espouse high confidence in being able to cure the patients' neurotic complaints; where "cure" does not mean absolute removal of symptoms but becoming able to live productively with them. Come to think of it, this kind of maturity is also valued in the Western way of thinking about human psychological difficulties, despite the often-advertised quick, total cure promised by advertisers of everything from flat feet to falling hair.

During this stay in isolation, the Morita patient is confined to a room alone, is given an explanation of his fundamentally psychological problems by the therapist, and is given "doctor's orders" to follow. The predicted course of treatment is that the patient will first (perhaps) enjoy his rest, then become restive, and bored with inactivity. This inactivity is significant: It is to prompt self-examination and to learn to accept the anguish of inactivity, thinking about his obligations to others and knowing that his struggles with himself will pass. The inactivity — the respite — is a precondition, so to say, for change; the ensuing battle arising from self-confrontations — when alone and meditative brings a lesson in forebearance, humility, and patience. Following this trial period the patient is permitted to gradually engage in activites around the "hospital," that is to clean the room and the like. The next day or two the patient is allowed to leave confinement and return to regular life. Reynolds says of his own experience as a Morita patient; "As I walked out of the clinic the colors and sounds of busy Tokyo burst on me with unprecedented freshness and vitality. It was a kind of rebirth" (p. 10).[14]

Morita treatment continues beyond the "bed rest" and confinement period. Making a diary of *activities* (not feelings!); responding to the therapist's daily reading and annotating of the patient's diary; sharing social and informal gatherings with others; talking with one's therapist; and reading Moritist literature. These take place in the hospital area. Not until the last period is the client released: The patient continues to read, discuss, interact with others, attempting to improve relationships, going on errands from the hospital and on group excursions. The patient begins to engage in formal ex-patient meetings, to receive the hospital magazine; the actual in-patient stay is about forty to sixty days.

In summary, Reynolds says: "If we ask (the patient) how he is getting along, he is likely to say that his symptoms have diminished only a little, but the important thing is that he has learned to work, socialize, and behave normally in spite of them . . . he has begun to see his anxiety as part of himself, not as an appended symptom" (p. 12).[15]

The "feelings" issue becomes important in understanding Morita therapy and in contrasting this therapy with prevailing American therapies. Morita therapy distinguishes clearly between feelings and behavior, the same way the present book has attempted to do in previous chapters (especially those relating to behavioral therapy). The Moritist hold that our behavior is under our control, our feelings less so, and the behavior becomes a *responsibility.* The patient is obliged, encouraged to "do it anyhow" even if s/he does not "feel like it." In American culture we countenance feelings too much and use them as excuses and ways out of dilemmas and conflicts; not so with the Japanese. The Moritist and the Japanese, far more generally than Americans, learn that best satisfactions come from doing and completing tasks, and that this attention to reality does not make of one a robot. One might say, "Doing a task does not one a robot make." The Japanese would agree.

One could go on describing Morita therapy, but this much introduction is sufficient to give the picture. It is strongly in contrast with much American "mental health instruction," if we may call it that, but at more profound levels we all know that to be comfortable, to feel well, we are obliged to do that which we are obliged to do. Reluctance, suffering therewith, anxiety, feeling rebellious or postponing . . . are all real *feelings,* to be sure, but not sufficient *reasons* not to do one's bidding. The old American statements: "Pull yourself together," "Get on the stick," "Try harder," and so on give occasional testimony to similarities to the Japanese/Moritist position. One trouble is, in American culture, much of the exhortation picture would be an irritant to patients/clients who have been instructed to hold that feelings are the end-all and be-all of mental health.[16]

As to researched effectiveness of Morita therapy, Reynolds reports some findings by two Japanese therapists – Suzuki and Suzuki (1977) – which indicate that of over 1,200 patients treated by their Morita clinic over a 10-year period, 71 percent returned follow-up questionnaires. One important reported result was that the greatest therapy impact came one to two years after the close of treatment (Reynolds, 1980, p. 45). We have to view these findings with some caution, however, as we do not know the total number of clients who applied or entered (and did not finish) treatment, and whether all participants, however tentative their cooperation, were included in the statistics. What attrition means in Japan has not been well studied; we know from American studies that this fact alone can sometimes greatly change the meaning of therapy outcome. It is, of course, possible that the Japanese with their great adherence to responsibility do, in fact, respond better to therapy, do follow-through, do answer questionnaires in greater numbers, and do not show as much attrition. Only more research will tell us the larger picture if there is one.

Naikan Therapy

Naikan therapy has Buddhist roots, as one might expect, but stems not from the Zen sect, but from the Jodo Shinshu sect appealing to the masses of people, not the warriors and aristocrats of the former sect. The particular faith promises that Buddha's love will draw the believer into paradise upon death. The strong religious backing for Naikan therapy is seen in the practice of the therapy itself, having been integral to the training of Jodo priests. In time, however, the Naikan movement has come to mean pursuit of self-understanding.

The practice of Naikan therapy is demanding. Its treatment versatility is, however, wide: Reynolds indicates that it has been applied to prison inmates as well as to people with family problems, neurotic and psychosomatic difficulties. Typically the treatment begins with a three to fifteen-day period in isolation; although abstaining from food, water, and sleep are not required, some practice this self-denial. Days of self-denial are long — from 5:30 A.M. until 9:00 P.M. — immersed in meditation. The patient is asked to direct his contemplation first to his mother, later to other members, remembering his preschool, elementary, and junior/senior high school periods. During this meditation, the sensei (therapist) comes to the patient several times a day, from one to two hours, and asks the client about his meditation. Both therapist and client interact in ritualistic form, bowing, being humble, and listening carefully to each other. The client reports to the sensei on what he, the client, has received from the person (mother, say) who is the object of his meditation; what he, the client, gave in return; the troubles the client caused the mother (or whomever). More emphasis is spent on the last theme, the trouble the client had visited on others. Reynolds observes that most clients report having received a lot, given little; as a result the client is guilt-ridden and remorseful. Reynolds reports the client may speak of suicide or dying. Repentance comes from learning from the therapist that despite the client's insensitive behavior, s/he was loved by his parents and family; this theme appears to lead to the client's renewed interest in life, in serving others, and repaying others. The chain of events may be described as: guilt — repentance — service to others — new meaning to life. These themes are, of course, known to the Western world, as found in the Judeo-Christian tradition of admitted guilt leading to repentance and a new life. It is interesting to note that, as Reynolds reports, the Naikan and Morita therapies have intended to disconnect themselves from their religious heritage and moorings; in the USA such therapeutic practices based on guilt, as cited above, would draw not only criticism but likely strong repudiation. Both American and Japanese therapies have intended to steer away from religious implications but have ended up in seemingly opposite therapeutic and philosophical situations, especially regarding guilt and its alleged tutorial value. This point brings up another significant one, viz., that most therapies — perhaps all of them (with the possible exception of much of behavioral therapy) — have arisen out of nonscientifically validated principles, mostly moralistic and culturally approved ones, some myth and some truth and honesty about human relationships, a conglomerative mix of factors. Therapy has been so much needed in the modern industrial world because of the stresses and strains of living, because of the inherent unfairness in the economic order, that they have sprung up with only temporizing features, sometimes hardened into doctrine (as with psychoanalysis) and have failed to study their own course and outcome. One way to interpret this statement is to say that "therapy is a mess," and the proliferation of therapies in the USA, plus the contrasting viewpoints in the Japanese mode, all give rise to the realization that therapies and therapists have a long way to go before they reach a state of stable dependence for the average person seeking help.

Reynolds' second book, *The Quiet Therapies* (1980), is the best overall description of the Japanese styles of psychotherapy. They have all grown up in, and out of, a culture with some striking differences between Japan and the USA. Yet there are some obvious and interesting overlappings; these require much more study if we are to understand each better, the American and the Japanese ways in therapy.

Back to Naikan therapy. The theory here stresses interpersonal relationships, especially that of the child with family and mother. The nexus of the problem in the family is not with instinct repudiation, or mistreatment by the parents, as in the American modality, but the offspring not appreciating what has been done for him/her. This leads to a self-centeredness, symptom formation, and suppression of the self-centeredness (not acknowledging its presence or potency in one's makeup). This latter point borders on the Freudian repression theory. But to get over this unwanted (a behavioral statement) state of affairs, the Japanese patient has to admit his/her selfishness and get on with recovery and recompense, a matter of a few weeks of intensive mediation, guilt, reformulation, and renewed zest. Here the similarity with the Freudian — and offshoot — models where the lack of recognition of selfishness takes not that direction but many, many others (all leading to different diagnostic categories and a complex nosology) and, in turn, requires years of intensive searching for the origins and reconstruction through a labrynth no one has ever been able to fathom or clarify. The Japanese model of neurosis causation and remediation (therapy) is much simpler, more socially-oriented, more easily treated, and asks for acknowledgement of wrongdoing and recompense in social ways; whereas the American depth model — and its derivatives — ask for a complete rebuilding of personality with not-too-much social implication (except secondarily).

Japanese and American psychotherapies (except for the behavioral position in the later) state that failure of therapeutic effort is the patient's fault, not that of the theory or practice of psychotherapy. They both appear to be equally vulnerable in this respect, in my view of things. One cannot, of course, as a therapist take full responsibility for a client, or for anyone else — the notion of personal responsibility as a social axiom is straightforwardly repudiated by this "therapeutic" notion — but one can take responsibility as a therapist for knowing how, or conceivably arranging, matters that can be put to the client's benefit. Behavioral therapists do this all the time in working in institutions of many kinds; in the one-on-one psychotherapy the environmental controls are largely lacking — for the behaviorist — and are of no consequence to the depth therapist. This whole area of individual (client) versus therapist (and societal) responsibility is also a mishmash of weak principles, strong belief, inconsistent practice, and socially negative theorizing. You now pays-your-money-and-takes-your-choice; not much enlightenment from science, society or sanity is forthcoming for the individual (or group) patient. This, then, is another area in which the leading edge of research is so desperately needed; it will be some time before we gain much clarity about the responsibility issue.

Other Japanese therapies include Shadan (an isolation or rest therapy); Seiza, a quiet-sitting therapy; and a Zen meditation therapy. All of these bear similarities to the Morita and Naikan positions, yet have their differences, too. In the USA we have at least 250-plus varieties of therapy, most differences being semantic, it would appear, and certainly not carefully researched positions; in Japan the number is far fewer, but the research stance is not much better, although the Japanese appear to try to do more follow-up research, therapy-by-therapy, than do the Americans. (See Reynolds, 1980, pp. 66-101 for more detailed discussion of these additional Japanese therapies.)

In summary among all the Japanese therapies Reynolds writes about, he makes some interesting points. One point is that Japanese therapists try to treat the *flux* in life, not the noun-adjectives that report us to be "good," "bad," "neurotic," and so forth (Americans are great on dichotomies, as we well know, and then to convert adjectives and verbs into nouns, into entities, into states, rather than seeing the flux). Different ways of treating this flux are points among the differences in the Japanese mode of therapies, whether to slow down the flux, let it go unhindered, try to redirect it, and so on. One focus in the Japanese therapy is to get the person to focus on others, away from self, away from self-consciousness and self-preoccupation. American therapies try this tact, too, but in such a variety of ways, bolstered by (alleged) theories, that one has trouble following what therapists do and what they mean by what they do. Talking is not as much emphasized in the Japanese therapies as in the American and European versions (was not Freud's contribution epitomized as being "the talking cure"?); as talking is properly seen as clever ways to dodge issues, to draw on too selected talked-about topics, and to meet social respectability and approvability criteria, rather than to change.

On the aims of therapy, Japanese and American (and Westerners, generally) part company: We in America stress happiness and as everyone knows we are backed up in this quest by the authenticity of the American Constitution — what better evidence of happiness, as a right, could we have? The Japanese may be somewhat more realistic in acknowledging more openly that life is full of pain, anger, sorrow, joy, and other strong emotional reactions; to try to deny or replace or summarily dismiss them is foolish, ill-conceived, and bound to fail. The Japanese Buddhist principles are more open and acknowledging about these vicissitudes, and part of therapy is adjusting to them, admitting or accepting them, and dealing more openly with them. There has been, of course, in the past decade or two, some "maturing" of the typical American attitude to, for example, death, where we say now that we must be more open about death and learn to deal with it as the natural outcome of life, rather than to go whistling along in the dark as if it would never occur *to us* (or to ones dear to us). There has grown up an American "new" attitude toward death recently, so we are getting in line more with the Japanese model (that not being our intention, however) and more with reality. Therapy is now considered to be mainly "supportive" of people caught in the anguish and sadness of death, not a posture that tries to place its significance backward in time in one's life, or set it aside, or other unrealistic positions.

However, the Japanese attitude of acceptance generally is more stabilizing than the ones we promote in America. We promote a hodgepodge of objectives and outcomes from therapy — they produce highly mixed results, by the way, when researched — and the Japanese want to teach, via therapy, that one may not rid himself of all pain and anguish, that these states are not "tacked on" to life, and that one's happiness, if you will, is not jeopardized by being realistic about life's shortcomings. One goes on and does what he is supposed to do — the sense of responsibility — in spite of not "feeling well" about it, and in spite of outright anguish and pain. This acceptance is not passive, it is not resignation, as many Americans would hold, rather it is simply *realistic*.

Some other features of Japanese therapy relate to bodily posture and the lack of mind-body dichotomy as with American thinking. To some extent, the traditional Japanese therapies are a bit like the "new" body therapies in the USA, but the theories underlying each are considerably different. Japanese therapy is somewhat related to the American notion of "resocialization" as Reynolds points out (1980, p. 107). The social skills movement, cited above, being a new outgrowth of the behavioral position, resembles the Japanese model of resocialization. This greater social interest and emphasis, together with the realism characterizing the general philosophical outlook of Japanese therapy (and what can be accomplished in therapy) points up both similarities and differences in Japanese and American therapy. A thorough analysis of their similarities and differences is not possible in this small space, but such a product would be advisable for patients, therapists, and theorists of psychotherapy. It will come in due time.

The overall emphasis in the Japanese therapies as "quiet therapies" is a most interesting and cogent point. American therapies are more active, generally, with behavioral ones being the most active and planful.[17] However, the Japanese therapies are not without plan; they are not aimless, but actually very highly structured — from the beginning in isolation, the assignments to meditation and topics related thereto, the gradual reemergence after periods of guilt and anxiety, and the active rehabilitation and follow-up characterizing the end points of therapy in the Japanese mode. Japanese theory is nonspecific; American theory of therapy sometimes strives for specificity. American "depth" therapy procedures (not the behavioral methods) are somewhat aimless and wandering; Japanese procedures are highly structured, even rigid by American standards. The progress of therapy is well-plotted by the Japanese, ours ranges from the national mean number of sessions of 4 to 8, out to hundreds of hours spread over many years. The aims of therapy, as we have seen, and the eventual outcomes are sadly lacking in both cultures, with very few exceptions. We all err on this count. The messages for the future of therapy are written in the ink of attrition, flow through the system, follow-up and relationships to the community of natural social support. (See Phillips, 1985, Chapter 3, reference 5 for a more complete exposition of this viewpoint.)

Some final comments on Japanese and American therapies in Reynolds (1980, p. 110) are appropriate here: "With few, minor exceptions, Western psychotherapy can be characterized as verbal exchanges aimed at elimination of symptoms. The Japanese therapies are marked by significant, long periods of silence aimed at acceptance, incorporation, and transcendence of symptoms." A good note on which to close this chapter and to move into the social arena more explicitly.

Chapter 6

SELF-HELP AND SUPPORT GROUPS

IN RECENT YEARS the popular aspects of the large scale mental health movement have also produced several grass roots movements. One of these has been the emergence of self-help groups, support groups, and the like. They go by different names, but their overall purpose, structure, and functioning seem similar.

Self-help and/or support groups are usually small collections of people who share common problems; they meet to discuss these problems on a periodic basis much the same as if they were in formal group (or individual) therapy. Often these groups are leaderless, but a kind of leadership emerges in the form of the more assertive people involved in them, or leadership may revolve around persons who first activate the group. Leadership appears to be less important than the fact that a few people are willing to take the time to share their concerns in a regular way; such meetings often are arranged for at the homes of the participants, in a church or some other public place allowing for such group meetings (as a community-supported activity), and at regular times.

These groups are usually formed among people who have gotten to know each other from a setting shared by most or all of the participants (church, recreational group, school, office). Rarely are members of self-help or support groups unknown to all the other membership, although as with any such constellation of persons, membership does change and degrees of participation fluctuate.

As part of the larger mental health movement — one might call it that — these support groups take the place of formal therapy to a considerable extent. Sometimes people move from formal therapy (either individual or group) to support groups for a variety of reasons — convenience, informality of the support group, general social sharing as well as specific concern over personal problems, little or no cost, and so forth — and sometimes they play forth and back between formal and informal sources of help (psychologists, psychiatrists, social workers, ministers, although the latter are seldom licensed to do psychotherapy). Occasionally people will leave informal support groups and engage in more formal therapy, preferring this route (although it is much more expensive, third party insurance payments account for about one-half up to 80 percent of the costs associated with formal therapy by a licensed practitioner), feeling that their problems are too serious or involved for the support group, preferring the one-on-one relationship, or thinking "licensed competence" is the hallmark of successful help with personal/emotional problems.

Support groups have taken a lot of directions. Some of them emerge as a kind of social/community/economic emergency such as getting an area of a city cleaned up, freed from rats, or flooding, or some other environmental problem. Some form to contest a governmentally neglected problem such as issues related to traffic flow near a school area, speeding on city streets, dumping garbage in nonlegitimate places, and the like. Others relate to shared social/personal/family problems such as Alcoholics Anonymous and the related Alanon support, arising from the alcoholic problem of one family member. Support groups, then, can arise to meet an immediate environment, family, or community problem; when their mission is accomplished, they tend to disband, Those forming for more personal problems such as emotional, social, and related issues in peoples' lives, tend to be less clear-cut in their missions, less obvious, more fragmented, and probably more elusive. That would apply to social support groups in the mental health areas, broadly conceived. These are the ones we are primarily concerned with in this book, those that supplement, augment, or replace formal individual and group psychotherapy.

While the idea of how a support or self-help group operates is pretty clear to most people, Levy (1976, p. 311) supplied this formal definition: Such groups ". . . provide help and support for its members in dealing with their problems, and in improving their psychological functioning and effectiveness."[1] This definition fits best with mental health types of issues, but it also can apply where community efforts are the main focus of change for both individual and groups in a neighborhood or city, for whatever reasons (environmental, social, ethnic, health, political, etc.).

Weber (1982, pp. 14-15) says (paraphrased) that the overall characteristics of self-help and support groups include the following: usually small, voluntary, often without any parent organization; members share common problems/interests/needs/experiences; may reject standard help sources or reject prevailing social norms; rely on face-to-face interaction; may disband when their purposes are fulfilled; may be refueled from time to time due to resurgence of issues, and membership may change over time with some leaving the group and new ones coming in.[2] Participation over time is not known, no groups having been researched (as far as the literature is concerned) for the attrition matter. We do not know, then, whether participation in the self-help and support group areas looks like client/patient participation in formal therapy (either among community clinics or among private practitioners).

The prevalence of self-help groups has seldom been surveyed. In the USA, the terrain is too vast to know what percentage of people engage in any kind of self-help or support groups; in local communities, however, the presence of mental health/psychological types of such groups are known to be common. In one setting I know about, 17 support groups existed at one time from among a total church membership of about 500-550 people. If such support groups averaged a membership (in actual attendance at most meetings, that is) of 5 to 10 people (a likely figure), that means that from 80 to 160 people (from 16 to 30 percent) of the total population of this church were involved in support groups of one kind or another (some about family problems, some about career interests, some about more strictly emotional and interpersonal issues), a figure much higher than those expected to consult with private mental health practitioners or community mental health clinics[3] (Veroff et al., 1981, pp. 75-87).

One important aspect of the support group and self-help movement has been the linking of national groups with one another. Once an idea shows viability in the self-help area, it is easily transported to other localities[4] (Stokes, 1981, pp. 131-133). The best example of this type of nationwide self-help group success is, of course, Alcoholics Anonymous. Many subsequent groups having to do with stopping smoking, losing weight, and support for various handicapped groups have followed in the Alcoholics Anonymous wake but not as successfully as AA. However, many of the nationwide support and self-help groups remain highly visible and make an impact on communities irrespective of the actual number of followers. The fact that extant programs exist is, itself, a humane and socially desirable influence; in time, or on occasion, people resort to them, sometimes for long periods, sometimes for only short periods of time.

Problems and Contraindications

Rybczynski[5] (1980) pointed out that small is not always beautiful and local is not always better. That is to say there are often problems with support group efforts, especially in the economic areas. Values of support groups may conflict with other community values. Some communities have suffered pollution problems with wood burning stoves, as an example. Sometimes support groups need places to meet and cannot command the attention of public sector buildings (schools, churches) without inviting political and ideological controversies, resulting in disfavor to the self-help organization. In the psychological self-help area, however, there are fewer constraints on organizing and on keeping the effort going. People become disenchanted with one another, fight over leadership roles, and invoke personal prejudices of one sort or another, but these kinds of constraints abound in all human activities, not alone with self-help efforts. Most people in the mental health areas appear to know well in advance that human interactional problems may arise and attempt to be prepared. There is nothing wrong with a support group splitting off and forming two groups, or three or more, if internal integrity seems to demand it. Several stories have come to me that indicate that mental health support groups will become divisive because some members want only to speak about husband-wife problems, or problems with children, when many of the group members are single and have no children. These groups have afforded better support for their members by splitting off and defining topics more clearly than just the need for support per se. Actually, such support groups tend to move in the direction of some behavioral types of intervention by defining at the outset what their goals will be. The original motivation just to get started with some kind of self-help or support organization has moved more into the arena of special help groups for special problems; the catchall nature of support groups has appeared to diminish in favor of more specific kinds of problems. Similarly, people in general support groups at first appear to need to migrate to more specific ones which take up issues of a limited nature (vocational choice and job change, dealing with aging parents, help with severely handicapped children, and so forth). The general nature of some generic forms of support groups can hardly deal with the highly specific problems with retarded children, autistic children, senile parents, and the like. Aside from the need for technical assistance in such cases, support group focus may have to deal with the members getting help from their own siblings (in the case of senile parents), dealing with unsympathetic and inadequate teachers in the case of handicapped children, and similar problems. Support groups can be of some help in these instances but are usually less effective in helping their members when the basic issues in living are technically involved well beyond the expertise and competence level of the support group.

The last observation — that of technical competence and expertise of the support group — raises an interesting and far-reaching problem. Can support groups of the mental health type actually deal with technical problems of, say, getting special classes for handicapped children started in the public schools (or inaugurating a private effort of the same sort)? The frustrations parents have had in getting help with and for exceptional or handicapped children are legion. Just supporting one another in the frustrations — in the sense that couples experience frustrations with one another — may not be enough; some more fundamental changes are indicated. Support groups may help ginger up the motivation for change, help members persevere, but the technical aspects of proper education for handicapped children abound and just supporting one another is not enough. On the other hand, more limited interpersonal problems between lovers, husbands and wives, parents and children, etc. may be highly responsive to self-help group participation and support. We simply do not yet know enough about the wide range of self-help groups and how they function, what their accomplishments are, and how long and viably they last, to be able to draw many conclusions about them. We do know, in a naive sense, however, that most support groups of a general nature *appear* to serve many of the purposes that individual, formal therapy serves, for many people; but we do not know the limits on those alternative kinds of social service. There is much need for wide-ranging research in these areas of human experience.

Perhaps aside from, and in addition to, the actual occurrence and continuance of self-help and support groups is the fact that individuals, in wide collections of instance, are learning that they can take many matters in hand regarding their personal lives. They need not sit home in social isolation, depressed about their plights, unknowing about others in similar straights, and unprepared to take even small advantages of existing sources of help. The self-help and support groups are quite able to help define problem areas for examination, to suggest ways of going about problem solving, to help maintain a support matrix which people can resort to on the basis of personal need, and they can hold up to the community the size of the problems in society which support groups purport to tackle. The example the self-help and support groups offer is, itself, a highly heuristic matter. Support group efforts are also democratic, strengthening the flexibility of a society that can rise to the occasion of special problem areas for its members. Institutions such as schools, hospitals, governmental agenices, and the like are of course the bulwarks of help in a complex society, but they cannot do everything for everybody on call; they are highly limited in many respects. Self-help and support groups fill in between the cracks of legitimate institutions, can change more readily than can institutions, and can get down to the grass roots more ably than can institutions. The self-help and support group movements of recent decades is an altogether positive movement and represents the glue of life for many people. It is a viable alternative to formalized help (especially in the mental health arena), and continues to be a kind of "school" or instructional base for democratic solutions to important personal and social problems not easily covered by existing institutions.

The psychotherapy profession has been under considerable attack in recent years.[6] Many publications — as well as the one you are reading right now — have taken to task the psychotherapy profession. Some of the critical vantage points include the following: Psychotherapy is oversold; various psychotherapies, although touted, to the hilt, are probably not much different from one another, except for the slight advantage behavioral methods (too often ill-defined) have over most other short-term methods; short-term therapy is as good as, or better, than long-term psychodynamic/psychoanalytic psychotherapy and far less costly; the overall national average for outpatient psychotherapy (as we have abundantly shown herein) is four to eight sessions; the "attrition curve" appears to apply to all psychotherapy persuasions and shows that people get some help right off, some take a bit more time, and some appear to take, even in the short-term setting, a comparatively longer period of time, reasons for which are not well-understood and poorly researched at this time; and so on.

If, then, formal psychotherapy is not all it is cracked up to be, why not put more emphasis on self-help and support groups, perhaps extending these offerings more widely in society to ever larger membership?[7] (Maguire, 1983, pp. 43-59). Why not hold the more formal therapy for the more refractory cases, for those needing perhaps more support and more expertise than regular support groups can offer? Why not study the whole matter more fully? Our government in recent years has seen fit to cut back on mental health and other humane measures of research and practical support, just at a time when industrial societies are becoming ever more entangled in conflict, prejudice, and misunderstanding, when society is becoming more fractionated into poor and rich, advantaged and disadvantaged. These changes, themselves, require more social support as bulwarks against anomie, drastic and sudden change, disenfranchisement, and the like. The body politic as a collection of institutions is sorely in the need of the filling-in-the-cracks that support and self-help groups can provide. All of the people needing help for psycho/social problems cannot be sent to individual practitioners, nor can they all be treated in formal therapy in mental health clinics. However, more could be treated in the latter if the staff of these clinics would give up their "depth" psychology interpretations and theories of human distress and get on with more effective short-term psychotherapy, individual, group, and family in nature. This change alone would improve the mental health delivery potential of the several hundred existing clinics throughout the USA. These clinics, in turn, could sponsor, consult with, help support, the natural, grass roots, self-help mental health groups that spontaneously form to fill in the gaps currently existing in mental health help.

The criticisms of the psychotherapy profession do not lead, logically, to abandoning this form of help; they lead to *expanding* it in more practical and socially useful directions. If the prevailing psychotherapy treatment mode in existing mental health clinics throughout the USA (and in many private ones, too) is four to eight sessions, then let us offer this limited help up front, articulately, and with purpose. Let us, then, follow up systematically on these people to see if they get along fairly well. Those who do not respond well to the limited time can be given more time — again within some feasible time limit — and/or be referred to support groups. As matters exist now, community mental health clinics and counseling centers on university campuses do not know really clearly where, how and/or what reasons they refer their not-to-be-served clientele; usually, to private practitioners — if the clients have insurance — only to be kept in the "depth" psychology mode, not to be given a more alert, practical, problem-solving and support-maintaining therapy.

Just what social factors will prompt changes in the present delivery system is hard to estimate or predict, but changes will come about because the present system is responding only partially to the widespread need, and it is responding in a kind of willy-nilly way, not with aplomb, aforethought, and research support. One possible source of prompted change in mental health delivery systems is related to third-party payments (insurance support). As these costs mount, support of a financial nature will diminish. There is some confusion, however, between mental health insurance support and general medical insurance coverage — the latter having grown astronomically recently, but the former having maintained a respectable level.[8] And, further, research has shown that short-term psychotherapy tends to cut down on general medical calls to clinics, in a prepaid delivery system (the Kaiser Permanente Foundation, see Cummings and Follette (1976), and Follette and Cummings (1967).[9] The two facts — lack of mounting mental health costs and their corresponding economical impact on more strictly medical services delivery — bode well for mental health service and research support.

Another stimulus for improvement in the formal systems of mental health service delivery will, of course, come from just what we are talking about here: The rise of self-help groups and support system. As these improve in visibility and viability they can be expected to have two kinds of influence on formal psychotherapy delivery systems (private and public): First, an influence characterized by absorbing some of the clientele that would normally go to the formal system of help; second, by influencing the formal system to develop more flexible policies and to reflect in their operation and in their referral-out system, more practices similar to those found in the informal support and self-help groups. That is, the informal system will provoke both internal and external changes in the formal mental health delivery system. But in order for this process to go forward orderly and economically, much more research will have to be made on how these influences are felt, how they are responded to by the formal system, where the referrals pay off and when and where they are symptomatic of an absence of change, and how the informal systems can, themselves, respond most favorably to the needs they purport to meet. This is a circular process with the feedback to the formal system from the informal system, and vice versa, tending to winnow out the superfluous elements and improve the efficiency and effectiveness of both systems. This kind of change will take some time; research efforts, properly placed, should enhance the expected changes between and among the two systems of treatment in the mental health arena.

A third influence will arise more gradually and reluctantly, viz., changes in the training of therapists from all professions (psychology, psychiatry, social work and perhaps the ministry) in short-term psychotherapy for individuals, groups, and families. This will, in time, allow clinicians of all types to be better prepared for a practical kind of psychotherapy; it will lead to the sloughing off of depth notions (which are held to be most inappropriate for short-term work, despite the rush into short-term therapy by some psychodynamic psychotherapists in recent years) [10] help to make research more meaningful to clinicians, the institutions in which they work and, of course, to clients who are the main beneficiaries of these expected changes in mental health delivery systems.

LOOKING AT PREVENTION

In the mental health field prevention has been a valued purpose, but little progress has been made toward prevention. When the community mental health movement started in the USA and when this movement got its most vigorous boost, one touted benefit was that it would prevent more serious problems, keep people out of hospitals, and lead to early detection of potential patients (people "at risk" as the term most apt to be used in this connection). It is not clear that any kind of preventive effort has worked very well. This does not mean that preventive work is unimportant; it means that it is exceedingly hard to do and usually comes into the picture after-the-fact.

An example of what is both good and poor about preventive work in the mental health area is an article by Comstock.[11] Comstock points up well-intended actions of the Parents Anonymous group which was formed to help parents overcome problems with abusing their children. Showing the need that was met by this organization, Parents Anonymous grew to over 1,500 chapters by 1982, from its inception a few years ago. The article stressed helping parents change their own self-concepts, gaining in ability to express feelings, being closer physically to children and touching them more often. In group meetings, Parents Anonymous members discuss how to accomplish these better aims with children. However, there are no data showing how these instructional matters actually reduce the number of abusive interactions, both physical and psychological. To be convincing to parents and to students of mental health movements, more data are needed; this is another area in which research has been overlooked or neglected. The mental health field does not need to stress its measures only verbally or in expostulations and exhortations read in the daily papers and in magazines and books; more substantive efforts need to be made, otherwise critics of the movements will dismiss genuine efforts after superficial examination. Members of the clinical community — psychologists, psychiatrists, social workers, and others — should perhaps step forward and assist grass roots organizations such as Parents Anonymous to collect the data they need to convince and exemplify how their work can be truly preventive.

Gottlieb (1982) and Gartner and Reissman[12] (1977) have both suggested ways in which professionals can assist self-help groups, one of which ways consists in better data keeping and more accurate research on their activities and outcomes therefrom. Professionals cannot barge in, however, and impose their expertise on self-help groups; the groups must begin by sensing their need for support data on their activities and then solicit the help of better research-trained professionals. Some initial research reported by Gottlieb indicates that researchers did help the spontaneous groups identify clusters of needs and did help them direct their interest and momentum toward beneficial ends (e.g., among 87 respondents from 175 solicited — about 50 percent — Gottlieb reports that 18 self-help groups were identified and categorized into several subsets: loss-transition groups, stress, and coping groups as examples). Having made this kind of distinction as to what people in the community need, the next step is to show how group meetings and programs can, in fact, serve the purposes for which they were formed, viz., reduce the risk of more serious mental health problems if support is not forthcoming.

Not only among grass roots, self-help and support groups has prevention been considered important, the whole movement of community psychology has also stressed prevention.[13] Korchin asks if we know enough to really proceed with accurate preventive work; from the looks of things in the community psychology field, a more technical field than grass roots and self-help work, we apparently do not know much about preventive work. Lacking in these areas are accurate baselines of how many people engage in various types of treatment programs; from that baseline we might determine how many return for more help, go on to more serious problems, require hospitalization, have the law come down on them or actually be incarcerated, and the like; none of these types of data bases is very widely extant. We speak of prevention more with fond hopes than with accurate examples of the effect.

It is important that preventive work be pursued nonetheless. While clinicians have had to yield to the refractoriness of curing or ameliorating severe psychoses — except for some recent control measures attributable to drugs — and take up the treatment of less mental health problems, they have not succeeded very well in this substitute activity as we have seen herein. Now the clinicians are being challenged at the grass roots level by self-help and support groups; they will have to carve out more viable roles for themselves as their psychotherapeutic expertise becomes increasingly challenged by the self-help movement. One way that clinicians working in the larger community (as distinct from hospitals) can be more effective is to use their academic/research training to better advantage, not see their work as being infringed upon by novices or by the laity, but as an opportunity to bring desperately needed knowledge and skill to the whole prevention problem which no other persons can do as well. And perhaps the best way for professionals to function effectively in this capacity is not so much to work broadly in the grass roots areas, but to identify particular self-help groups that need research expertise, groups that have needs that are not being met by the general mental health movement, and yet are small enough to be well-described and researched. I am thinking of such groups as the PA (Parents Anonymous) groups dealing with child abuse, with groups tackling problems related to epilepsy, the study of the "little people of America," and the like[14] (see Borman et al. for further discussion of these populations).

Self-Help and Theories of Personality and Behavior Change

It should be apparent that looking to the community to help itself, found in and among the various self-support groups cited, that the traditional theories of personality and behavior change are not appropriate for this model. Self-help groups in many ways have little to learn from traditional personality theory, traditional psychotherapy (especially of the "depth" genre), and have begun to learn these lessons for themselves. The shock with this realization is being felt by the professional community, not by the grass roots membership. If personality and behavior change were so onerous and formidable as the traditional psychodynamic/psychoanalytic clinicians have held, no grass roots, self-help, or support group phenomena would be possible. Obviously the self-help groups have gained credence, visibility, and some viability; although their work has not been well researched, as we have amply indicated. The movement is too vast and too profound to stop and wonder about personality change in the manner discussed by traditional psychologists, psychiatrists, and others. The grass roots changes and their philosophy can well do without much of the vast range of clinical help in the psychotherapy field, with a few exceptions; and what the self-help movements need is not personality theory, or expensive treatment, but help with improving their work, researching its pros and cons, and generally spreading the word; reserving the most formidable cases for the expert clinicians, and some work by clinicians with self-help groups in order to increase the value and expertise of each. This is a vastly different program from what has been extant for decades, viz., the emphasis on grass roots and self-help efforts as "Band Aids" and not to be taken seriously; and the notion that effective change has little to do with the environment but is already inherently a matter of "depth" psychology and its formidableness.

Chapter 7

INTERCULTURAL AND OTHER CULTURAL THERAPIES

NOT ONLY are therapeutic matters within our culture of vast importance, as has been pointed out, cross-cultural and intercultural matters are also of use in understanding more about psychotherapy, especially short-term efforts.

Most Western cultures have their psychotherapies — we have referred already to some Japanese therapies — but none of them, occidental or oriental, has experienced the proliferation found in the USA. America, being the cultural melting pot that it is, has experienced a different kind of mixture in regard to psychotherapies; one of these mixtures is attempting to use the common modes of therapy on subcultural groups who have different backgrounds: For example, the intercultural problems in bringing therapy to black people, to Hispanics, to American Indians, and to recent comers to the USA from Europe and other parts of the world. These intercultural blends appear to require somewhat different therapeutic postures. The kinds of problems presented by blacks, by Hispanics, and so on, while overlapping somewhat with the standard white, American culture, also harbor important differences. Some of these differences are far-reaching in regard to morals, ethical considerations, family beliefs and practices, attitudes toward education, law, and the like. It has always been recognized that therapists should not impose their standards on their clients, even when these clients come from the same cultural background as the therapists; it is all the more important that the therapists, or the mental health agencies offering services, not impose traditional standards and values on the culturally different clientele.

Intercultural matters refer mostly to people who make up subcultural groups different from the main or standard American culture. As mentioned, blacks, Hispanics and others are — and are expected to be — different from middle class, American whites. Other cultural matters are concerned with comparing the therapies indigenous to different cultures or nations, whether they have blended or not. For example, culturally different therapies are the Japanese varieties — as we have seen — and they have not yet blended in with American varieties either in the USA or in Japan.

There is a vast literature (too lengthy to be covered here) on the intercultural problems associated with psychotherapy offerings in the USA. Most of the problems and prejudice against adapting therapy practices to subcultural groups arises in connection with American blacks. The second most distinct set of conflicts in how therapy is offered relates to differences between American whites and Hispanics. Some of the ways in which these intercultural differences bring about problems are the following.

Minority groups such as blacks and Hispanics are often less verbal than the white, middle class American. Therapists expect these subcultural or minority persons to be as verbal and ready to engage in self-disclosure as do whites. There are considerable differences here, leading to therapists being accused of not understanding the minorty member, and the minority member being accused of not being "ready for therapy." These communication logjams create a number of problems resulting in minority members not consulting mental health clinics (or private therapists, unless they speak the subculture language) since they feel misunderstood and not accepted. Also the "dropout" rate for some minority groups appears to be higher than for whites, although these kind of figures are very unreliable when the overall attrition curve, from a variety of clinics, is taken into consideration[1] (Phillips, 1985). However intuitively attractive it is to assume that (say) black/white therapists treating black/white patients will show substantial differences in therapy outcome, it is not borne out by research. Research results show a mixed bag: Overall, no consistent differences between these pairings of therapists and clients.[2]

Minority members, often being less well-placed economically, are unable to accept and pay for private psychotherapy. This practice is just not within their purview since they often lack insurance coverage and the kinds of jobs that would offer this kind of benefit. Traditionally, lower class people of both white and nonwhite origins, get referred more often to mental hospitals, are given medical treatment, and are not considered good psychotherapy risks, a fact that has been known for decades in the USA.[3] More recent literature has tended to confirm these earlier findings but with a bit more detailed information on how these prejudices influenced participants.[4]

An important factor in sizing up intercultural matters regarding psychotherapy, especially in the USA is that basic attitudes toward mental health — even aside from psychotherapy — are culturally based.[5] These attitude differences, even among youth of high school age, have been found, and they extend to American-Greek, American-German, and other ethnic/national background differences.[6] Any culture is likely to have its own belief system and in turn the belief system will likely influence whether people appear at all for therapy and how well they participate if they do seek help. In some "primitive" societies — better, developing countries — their therapies tend to center strongly on the individual, per se, as, indeed, Western therapies have done, and especially Freudian therapies in their earlier days in Europe.[7] For example, some shaman look into the eyes of the disturbed one to detect what is wrong and then set in with some kind of incantation to produce a remedy. Are not some "modern," individualistic therapies — those that place so much emphasis on the Oedipal complex, for example — similar in thinking to the shaman's notions? In contrast, those therapies that see the individual in a *social context* are very different from the "primitive" therapies and from the therapies in the Western world that look for specific causes "in" the individual.

What, then, do we learn from considering these other-world therapies? We see how we in the "modern" world have actually imitated these less scientific beginnings and have not, in some ways, moved very far beyond them. We see by looking at other cultures what is similar and different in our therapies and how much our therapies are reflections of the culture (which they may have to be) and not fully "objective" or "scientific" in the grander sense of these terms. It would be interesting to borrow some of the incantations from developing societies and try them out on members of our culture seeking psychological help; we might be surprised at the results!

OTHER CULTURAL THERAPIES

This section refers to psychotherapies from other cultures irrespective of their interactions with or within, the American culture. According to Tseng and Hsu, (1979),[8] the various psychotherapies of the world can be classified as mainly supernatural, natural, medical-physiological and sociopsychological. Mostly American psychotherapy is sociopsychological, although there are strands that believe in and practice medical-physiological psychotherapy (mainly through drugs). The developing countries may lean more toward the supernatural; and other modern cultures are more likely to be characterized as naturalistic and sociopsychological but with different content from American psychotherapy (Japanese therapy, for example).

Asian therapies, as has been shown with Japanese Morita and Naikan therapies, are more likely to be based on strong cultural values and beliefs and not be (individually) historically-oriented as are many American therapies. Like other cultures, Asian therapies are rooted in philosophical and religious beliefs historically prominent in a culture, and tend to state related views of man, his place in the world, and the importance of particular relationships in the culture.

While British therapies have many elements in common with the USA, there are also differences. Diagnostically, the British appear to diagnose "schizophrenia" less often than do Americans.[9] The British have never embraced psychoanalysis/psychodynamic psychotherapy as much as have the Americans. The British practice psychotherapy less than the Americans, having far fewer community mental health clinics than we do. One could not characterize the British and Americans as far apart, however; it is a matter of emphasis and of diversity that separates the USA and Britain in psychotherapy attitudes. In relation to the latter point, in America popular accounts of psychotherapy abound in the press, the theater, and in both humorous and serious literature. In the USA psychotherapy has become a kind of bread-and-butter account of social and interpersonal relationships — a kind of norm-setting is noted — but not so in Britain. How else would the USA have spawned over 250 varieties of psychotherapy, so-called? The Japanese hardly speak of differences in psychotherapy "schools" and neither do most other nations. German psychology, if we are to follow the workings of the European Association of Behavior Therapists, is mostly behavioral and experimental, with psychotherapy being a close follower of this model. I have had many discussions with professional people from other countries, both Occidental and Oriental, and have been asked many times "Why?" or "How come?" we have such an emphasis on psychotherpay and so many varieties in the USA. Why so much emphasis on psychotherapy? they ask. Others have trouble understanding what psychotherapy is supposed to accomplish compared to ordinary interpersonal and social relationships. There is not as much puzzlement in other countries as to why and how people have difficulties, except possibly for the sometimes mysterious ways "hysteria" is viewed.[10] What is needed in this vague and far-reaching topic, (that of how psychotherapies are differently viewed and practiced throughout the world) is more intercultural comparative studies and research. In comparing the USA with Japan, Reynolds has made and published some interesting findings.[11] One finding is that there are far more men in formal psychotherapy (Morita and Naikan therapies, for example) than women, which may reflect not psychopathology but cultural pressures on men to achieve and almost the opposite pressures on women not to compete. We might say in the USA that this trend is almost the opposite; especially in university populations where women appear to outnumber men in seeking mental health help on a three-to-two basis.

The kinds of research and comparative studies needed, interculturally, could begin with simple statistical head counts: How many men and women engaged in psychotherapy? Are children referred for help? If so, are these referrals mainly to private practitioners or do they relate to schoolwork, developmental problems, and the like? How long does psychotherapy last, on the average, in different countries? There are countless numbers of similar questions that should be studied before people launch into the "theories" of psychotherapy which have never proven of much value in the USA (so why should they be important elsewhere?), save for behavioral interventions. Much better data that would help understand the culture as well as psychotherapy, per se, would come from very objective, statistical counts. These will come along in time but now they are lacking, thereby limiting our understanding of our own psychotherapy as well as that of others.

Chapter 8

ENVIRONMENTAL FACTORS: THE NEGLECTED PERSPECTIVE

OF THE VAST ARRAY of psychotherapy offerings – well over 250 of them! – most of them locate the significant variables (the presumed causal factors that account for psychological disturbances) in the "psyche." That is, they say the difficulties are "in" the individual in some obscure way; theories accounting for the "inner" problems are therefore legion. They may include the Id, Ego, and Superego trichotomy of Freud, the "racial unconscious" or the archetypes of Jung, and more. They may include the "mental" states of cognitive/behavioral psychology and psychotherapy. All of these inner states are said to ramify in various ways and directions, disaffecting the individual's capacity to function.[1]

There are probably lots of reasons psychological theorists of all sorts have resorted to the "inner" explanations. We all experience subjective states; we all seem to note that we think about something, then do it. We tend to observe, we aver, that what seems to go on inside of us is perforce, first, foremost and the cause of our overt behavior. Our everyday language supports these common sense observations: "I will *think* it over." "I didn't *think* about that!" "My *feeling* is that it should be that way." These commonsense, natural language habits tend to direct our conceptualizations about human behavior and to offer seemingly causal explanations of how and why we behave as we do, locating the source or cause of our behavior inside.

Our culture, broadly speaking, supports the "inside" theory, too. Plays, novels, poems, fiction of all sorts, and so on, probe the "depths of our thinking and feeling" and pay very little attention to our environments except in a secondary sense. The model view of human behavior from the arts is that they all express what's inside people. Even artists who expostulate about what they write, paint, sculpt, etc., think of the innovations as coming from their imagination or some other inside-the-psyche location.

Many of the postulates offered by psychotherapists also locate the most salient factors inside the person. Rogers has written extensively, as have other therapists, that the potential for change is inside us; if we understand how we feel and think, we will gain control; if we use our inner resources, we can solve our problem. It all comes from within us, we are told by Rogers and countless others.

Let's examine the "inside" notion a bit. One could argue philosophically that the inside/outside distinction is arbitrary and ultimately meaningless. What's inside is also outside; and perhaps vice versa, or propositions to be valid have to appeal to both directions, one might say. If we ask people — in therapy or just in everyday social exchanges — how they happened to feel or think as they do, they would tell you of some experience they had, or would be able to validate some significant experience if one carried the discussion far enough. Although people often qualify their thinking/feeling reports by saying, "I don't know why I feel (think) that way but I do" one can trace down the referents in the person's life with relative dispatch. I had one patient who always began her therapy session with a general broadside like, "I'm feeling terrible and I don't know why . . ." whereupon I would ask her a couple of questions about what went badly for her and in a few minutes we would have isolated the precipitants of her "bad feelings." The occasional perplexity people report about understanding how and why they feel (or think) as they do can readily be reduced to facts; but it also represents a general assumption they hold that they should not have to feel badly (shades of Albert Ellis' emphasis on people following the *shoulds, oughts* and *musts* of life so excessively)! If I *shouldn't* be inconvenienced, if I *ought* to be loved and appreciated and accommodated, then it is perplexing to me that I do have these disappointments. It is an easy step for the person — patient or not — to aver, "I just don't know why I feel so badly."

It is very understandable in this connection that the behaviorist asks the person questions about how the feeling might have come about, what precipitants have possibly been operating. I have never taken one's feelings at face value, in myself, or in my patients, for as long as I have known about the general behavioral position, but have always taken the feelings/thinking report as something to locate in time and space in the person's description of his/her activities and interactions. One of the most important aspects of therapist-client exchange in therapy is to locate the antecedent circumstances that might reasonably be connected with how the person feels or thinks about something, especially if it is a perplexing something. When the "depth" psychotherapists alleges that people need-to-get-in-touch-with-their-feelings-more, I answer that they are already in touch with their *feelings* (and even overwhelmed and perplexed by them), and the problem is that they are not in touch with the circumstances (broadly speaking) which account for the feelings. Feelings do not exist in a vacuum; they always represent some outcome from experience, some pronouncement, some pro or con, something agreeable or not (or possibly neutral), and are not entitites in their own right. If a therapy simply probes feelings, it will get less far than if it takes the feelings (and thinking) as a beachhead from which to explore more of the terrain, a terrain that is full of accounts of how the person has *behaved,* how others have *behaved* toward him/her, and so forth. This point about how the client and others behave toward each other comes to life immediately when the client is asked, "And what did s/he say to you?" . . . and "How, then, did you handle this yourself . . .?" And so on. This tact leads to productive exchanges by the client between one's environment and one's evaluations of experiences with the environment. All feelings arise in connection with some interactions with the animate or inanimate environment; they don't blow in from outer space.

It is very important, then, to help clients/patients see themselves more appropriately within the context of their environments. One of the important questions about changing things for the better among all of us, patient or not, is that we might try to arrange our environment to better suit our purposes, to minimize friction or discomfort, or the like. If we get up 10 minutes earlier, we progress better through traffic to our destination; starting late causes us to become irritated — especially early in the morning — with traffic snarls and delays, and we reach our destination all worn out, *not feeling well.* This is an obvious example; in much of real life, the connections between some of our behaviors and some of our feelings is not always so clear; part of therapy is spent in making the search, the connection between feelings and behavioral events, *and then doing something about them.*

Several psychologists have captured this inside/outside, person/environment, fairly cogently. Ellis, e.g., speaks of the ABCs of disturbances, with (A) being the Activating Event; (B) the person's individual Belief System that the Event impinges on; and (C), the emotionally charged Consequences . . . One can see immediately that there has to be an Event — something happening in the personal or impersonal environment of the client — which, then, has "meaning" to the person in some particular and significant way (B), that produces a response (anger, disappointment, depression, surprise, etc.) by the person which, also, is significant; giving rise to (C), the matter that disturbs the person, brings him/her to therapy, and so on. Note how much the environment plays a role here — in the *event* and in the *consequences* which affect the client's behavior and interpersonal relationships with others. Although Ellis puts most of his emphasis on (B), the emotional reaction, an "inside" matter, the provoking circumstances and the consequences are very behavioral; and, also, the (B) is behavioral although its locus seems to be subjective, because it causes one to be moody, withdrawn, covertly angry, and so forth, as part of the feeling base. We could say that like a train that starts above ground, goes underground then reemerges to the above-ground surface, the ABCs of Ellis are highly behavioral; even the (B) part has a periscope, so to say, connecting feelings with behavior and social events "above ground," before the feelings culminate in their consequences — the train above ground — and its impact on the person's relationships to his/her environment. Without the behavioral, environmental anchorage points, the "inside" part of Ellis' formulation would not mean much; it would have no connections with anything in the world. It is just this lack of seeing the connections-with-the-real-world that perplex and confuse; and allow us, willy-nilly, to stay "underground" looking there for causes and remedies instead of opening up the train of events that sandwich in, so to say, the personal/subjective/emotional aspects.

Behavioral psychologists have a similar formulation: Also, the ABCs of disturbance, but stated a bit differently: (A) = the Antecedent Event(s), similar to Ellis; (B) the response, reaction, effect-on-the-person; and (C), the consequences. The (B) in the behavioral formulation – except with cognitive-behavioral formulations – is Response, Reaction, whether felt and reported by the client, observed by others, or both. The behaviorist does not go "inside" to account for, study, or explain the (B) portion of this chain of events; it is treated as are any other aspect of the chain; one does not enter a different world with (B) in the behavioral formulation. In fact, some effort in behavioral therapy is meant to make the (B) portion as explicit and objective and open-to-change as possible, but the emphasis is not put exclusively on the (B) as the explanation of (C) (or (A)). If one has the familiar elevator phobia, the (B) portion in treatment might be broken down into gradations, approached through successive approximations, *in vivo* or vicariously so as to make better connections with the real world in which elevators (or other important or critical phenomenon) exist. Philosophy of science scholars have dealt with these issues for decades, or longer[2] that is, issues revolving around the relationship between subjective experiences (of, say, phobia for elevators), versus actually going to the elevator to work out the problems. The subject matter of psychology is like the subject matter of *any* science; it is a matter of scientific labor, or how one or another science uses some methods particular to its own field; but it is not an issue about subject matter, per se; rather, how the subject matter is studied.

One of the reasons long-term therapy, the "depth-probing" varieties, take so long is that they state that they have to find the origins in experiential terms – the original "trauma" or whatnot that gave rise to the problem – and this understandably takes time; from a behavioral standpoint it is a will-o-the-wisp approach, neglecting the immediate environmental contingencies associated with the continuance (maintenance) of the person's difficulties. What keeps the difficulty alive, so to say, is not the extent of the original trauma (even supposing there was such a subject matter to be found and investigated) but all the surrounding conditions that currently – or of recent vintage – that help keep the disturbances going.

I can relate an experience I had recently in a New York airport awaiting a flight. I spent the time reading and observing people. Two families had young children, toddlers, who were, of course, into everything. One mother was constantly hovering over the toddler, admonishing him to do, or not do, this or that, swooping down upon him to protect him from some expected harm or nuisance, and hardly a minute went by when she was not imposing herself and her regulations on the child. Occasionally he would cry and squirm in apparent protest. Another family had a child about the same age; and the mother (and father) were quietly following the child around, unobtrusively, gently steering him away from the flower pots that had used chewing gum, paper, and other trash in them, and talking with him about what he had come upon in his explorations, giving him full access to crawling, rolling on the floor, walking, holding on to objects, and so forth. The contrast between the two families was striking.

Now let us assume this sample of the two families' behavior vis-a-vis their respective male toddlers were to continue for years and we see them entering first grade. The former toddler might be anxious, furtive in his relationships, oppositional toward teacher and other children (protesting the hovering and interfering of his mother over the years); the other child would be expected to be more calm, relaxed, confident, exploratory, inquisitive, cooperative, because he had had an *environment* compatible with his growth and potential. He had a nurturing environment, the former child a somewhat oppressive environment. These two contrasting environments might be expected to shape or direct the two children very differently. What, then would a therapist examine if and when the two children were the subject matter of study, for therapy or not? Would the therapy of the "oppressed" child (at schooltime or as an adult) have to go back and examine all the intricacies of the past? Who would report them? Who would see the child as I did in the short sample in the airport, for whatever it was worth in studying the emotional climate of the child's home and family? Would not a therapy that identified a too anxious mother, too interfering, too oppressive, etc. not be the tack to take therapeutically? Would not the mother of the first child have to learn more relaxed ways to discipline, educate, and monitor her child? Could not this be done by setting up examples from everyday living, a kind of log of interactional patterns (both "good" and "bad") between the first mother and her child? Would not an economical therapy emanate from the kinds of observations I made (originally) in the airport but also made current (at treatment time) in the family life of the "disturbed" child? What would we find if we tested the first child? What would probing his "psyche" tell us? Both — formal testing and projective (indirect testing, projective techniques, play products such as from coloring and drawing, and the like) — would reveal that the first child was "anxious," "withdrawn," "unsure of himself," "competitive with other children," or maybe the opposite, shrinking from self-assertiveness, owing to anticipating being criticized or scolded.

Even if the first child (in play therapy, as a testing technique) used the "mother doll" to scold the "boy doll," and similar projective revelations, we would know from our example they were highly likely anyway. We would do well to let the child exhibit some of these tendencies, to be sure, (his feelings), in therapy, but more importantly, to help the parents set up new arrangements with the child somewhat different from those that have been described (their in-the-airport practices) and as having been hypothesized to be the background of the first toddler's later problems. Changing the interpersonal (family) environment would go much farther in helping this child to overcome difficulties than neglecting these family issues and concentrating, instead, on how the child felt about it all. The child felt badly about it all — we know that. You and I would feel similarly. Why belabor this point? Why test and test and test this point? Why probe the "psyche" endlessly? Why not use the time and energy to change the environment in salient and practical ways? That would do much better for the child and simultaneously help the parents who were the misinformed persons in the first place, although they were probably doing the best they knew how (and are not to be blamed in some accusatory, guilt-ridden sense), given their tensions, their informational base about children, given examples from their own childhood and so on. We have to treat this whole complex as a kind of "natural set of occurrences, given the conditions described" and so we want to be economical and efficient about it. Behavioral intervention would ask more of the "right questions," and produce discernibly efficient and effective outcomes — or not — and then be subject to confirmation or change, whichever would be indicated. Everything would be "up front," testable and in the hands of the cooperative effort by both therapist and client (or, in the case of children, the child's parents or other responsible adults).

No matter how much we introspect about ourselves, or help patients to introspect, under the assumption that the nuclear problem is "within," the environment is always intricately and integrally involved. All events have surroundings, so to speak; they all have a context, no matter what scientific subject matter we are studying, no matter what kind of therapy we are professing to use. Those "surrounds" are the larger issues and the issues that have to be taken into consideration if change is sought, or if understanding — along with change — is sought. I have never seen a patient who, complaining as s/he might about treatment from either or both parents, that that patient didn't exhibit some of the same behavior (toward others) that were attributed to the parent. The patient — the complaining one in this case — had learned some of the same unwholesome behaviors they felt the parent visited on them (the patient); that behavior now "belonged" to the patient. Once the present patient/client can size up his/her behavior in comparison to the parental behavior, that helps to objectify the behavior characterizing the present client, helps him/her make more deliberate and controlled choices about behaving similarly, and gives the client a leg up on self-control through self-monitoring. *That* kind of procedure is short-term therapy; *that* is what is meant by behavioral therapy; *that* is taking the environment into basic consideration as the baseline of events that gave rise to the present need for therapy and as the baseline of activities that keeps the problem active until it is solved.

The Adult's Environment

It is very easy to argue that the child's environment, as in the above examples, has a strong determining effect on the child's development, later personality, and possible psychological problem status. But what about the adult? Is not his/her environment more set by the time s/he is adolescent, or even earlier? How can environmental changes be made for the adult that are constructive?

The individual adult does live and function within a largely set environment. But many small matters can also loom important. Where one lives, the people one associates with, the manner in which one lives by his/her expressed values (usually involving other people), and the way one spends leisure time are all considerations. Working environments are also very important, as the recent literature on stress indicates. Close interpersonal relationships sometimes figure decisively as part of one's environment, as everyone will agree. The difficulty in rearranging any of these environmental matters is identifying what is the most significant part that needs to be changed. If we thoroughly dislike our jobs, this easily becomes a focal point; but some other environmental changes are less easily identified and may take greater effort to change.

A fairly straightforward approach to changing an environment may be seen with students. They often study amidst others' talking, playing music, moving about, and generally making confusion. Students often stay up very late in order to get the quietude needed for study, but that makes them risk oversleeping in the mornings and being late for class, going off without breakfast, and practicing generally poor health habits. If one says to stressed students that different living patterns are worth consideration, this may come as a surprise; they often think that whatever they do, how they spend their time, are all just "natural" ways of living. But if those ways of living are somehow detrimental, or cause people to use their time and talents less well, they constitute areas for change. In putting changes into operation, one rearranges his/her environment to some extent. "I never go home from the library until 9:00 P.M. any more because my two roommates create such confusion earlier around dinner time that I can't get anything done," one student said. She had altered her study time and place — now using a study carrel in the library — the current semester and was both doing better in schoolwork and feeling better about it. Another student changed his working time at a nearby hotel so he could have some study time while on the job and acquired a quiet room for sleeping when not on duty. Still another student arranged to go to his parental home each weekend to use the family computer and other equipment which he could never find available on campus or could not arrange his time when computers were available. These may seem like trivial instances of rearranging one's environment but they are not; small changes may have ramifying consequences for one's feelings about self, accomplishment, and social relationships.

One should have specific times and places for doing a lot of life's routine requirements: shopping, studying, taking care of laundry/cleaning/car care, and so forth. People who complain about ". . . not having time to do it . . ." are not people who are actually overworked as much as they are not planful. Watching TV in the evening can come *after* one has written the checks, letters, and made the grocery list; the TV comes as a "reward" for having done the necessary tasks, otherwise one does not get the tasks done, feels guilt about it, enjoys the TV less, and is fretful with him/her self. Children need to be taught early that study and homework come before TV and other recreational pursuits, otherwise self-discipline is not learned.[3]

A common mistake many people make is to think they require some ideal setting for the accomplishment of what they say that they "want" to do — write, play a musical instrument, paint, crochet, tend a garden. Most of these activities do not take a lot of time, but if one idealizes the activity and the time it takes, one can spend a lot of time waiting for the ideal setup and come off not accomplishing anything. Almost any hobby can be easily maintained at a fairly high level several times a week by just choosing an appropriate hour or two for these activities. Almost any social or other commitment can be taken care of in just a few hours (or less) each week: Helping out at a church, a charity, going for some swimming or other exercise, etc. Most people fret away more time than they ever use gainfully in their leisure.

I have never seen a seriously disturbed person who did not use his/her time poorly. Poor use of time is often a prelude to conflict between what one wants to do and what one actually does. One can say that the emotional disturbance brought on the ungainful use of time, but that is not the main cause; it may be aggravated consequence of poor living habits, but the main issues stem from chronically poor use of one's time and energies. When one gets better, emotionally speaking, one has begun to conquer one's time and energy expenditure; that is why simple behavioral measures can often make a real difference in one's integration, happiness, social effectiveness, self-esteem and all the other "goodies" arising from effective living.

A recent article appeared in the Washington *POST* on the subject of "Frustration,"[4] allowing it to be a common and compelling problem. A list of 50 items was cited in the article as common instances of frustration. Probably close to half of these 50 items revolved around use of time and effort — low achievement, poor planning of time, lack of weight/sleep/eating self-control, feeling unorganized, failing to exercise regularly, lacking follow-through on duties and obligations, vowing to improve one's effort because of feeling poorly about these matters, and so on. All common items; all common contributors to poor mental and emotional health (if not done), all avenues to constructive change if applied properly. And changing these sources of "frustration" are all examples of some kind of environmental control, (reassessment, rearrangement, and the like). We feel these lacks "within us," as we say, but that is not really where the lack is; it is, rather ***between us and our environment*** (or environments, since we have different environments for different purposes, and some of them we deal with better than others). Picking any items for change in this *POST* article would require some environmental change; the change could not take place "wholly within us." in the intropsychic sense. If we try to do it that way — the "inside" route — we are likely to be even more frustrated. Realizing that we are part of our own environment and that different factors in the environment are salient for this or that consideration, will help us go a long way in maintaining good mental, emotional and social health.

Chapter 9

TAKING OVER FOR YOURSELF (AND WHO NEEDS MORE THAN SHORT-TERM HELP?)

FOR AGES most therapists have agreed that the beginning of therapy should also make one aware of the end of therapy. We start in order to finish — not to go on forever. Some therapists began to set time limits back in the 1940s, in fairly systematic ways. Even early Freudian therapy lasted about six months to one year at, however, an intense rate of 4 to 6 times a week; but it was not the long-term therapy it is today. Keep the end-of-therapy in mind when starting therapy.

You can take over for yourself in a number of ways where therapy is concerned. Some of them are as follows.

First, choose a short-term therapist. You can do that by asking friends; calling mental health agencies in your community; calling university psychology, psychiatric and social work departments; by going to the library and looking up books on short-term therapy (also look under "time-limited" therapy, psychotherapy generally, and under psychology and psychiatry topics); and by calling the national (or state) associations of the professions of psychology, social work, and psychiatry. Most local professional organizations have referral research for the caller and can often tailor your request to where you work or live, with respect to preference for a male/female therapist, tell you about cost, as well as short-term orientation of therapists, and other information.

Second, obtain books on short-term or time-limited therapy from the library and read them, and make up your mind as to whether you feel some compatibility with what the author(s) write; even call or write to them if you have important questions the book itself does not answer.

At the library, also, you can look in the *Reader's Guide* for articles on therapy. Any librarian can help you with this quest if you are not used to using library resources.

Once you get a book on short-term therapy, consult the reference or bibliography sections for names of books and articles covering some specifics of short-term therapy that may interest you: depression, moodiness, handling anger, dealing with frustrations, and so forth. Zeroing in on what you think your main problems or complaints are will get you started in reading what is immediately salient to yourself.

Third, an activity you can carry out for yourself whether you engage in formal therapy or not, is to make a daily log of how you feel, what seems to start off your feeling (waking up depressed in the morning, for example, but gaining momentum during the day, and so forth), and any related items you can identify as possibly contributing to your distress. Add, also, to this list of feelings and their possible antecedents, the *consequences* of your feeling – did you withdraw? Take a drink? Call a friend? Go for a walk? Sit in a stupor? And so forth. You will have conducted your own "ABCs" of functioning: the antecedent conditions, the problem behavior/feeling/thinking itself, and the consequences. If you go into therapy, this ordering of your experience will help you get started, set goals, define time limits, and judge how well the therapist(s) you see will be able to help you. If you are prone to consult a willing friend, this ordering of the distress may also be helpful to you.

The *fourth* thing you can do is seek out some support group or groups and go to them on a "look-and-see" basis. Sometimes support groups are a bit incongenial to outsiders, so you may not always get a warm welcome; some will not accept you as a visitor, and some will welcome you, especially if you have a personal entree. Judge how well the support group can be of help, especially if it meets often enough to satisfy what you think are your needs, and if the members seem available at other times for a chat and/or a "consultation." Sometimes the support groups are a source of information about formal therapists; you might come up with a good, personal recommendation for a therapist through a support group member, and you might avoid unproductive efforts at finding a therapist.

You may consider attending a support group as well as seeing a therapist. In interviewing members of support groups, I found that they all felt the group was just that, very supportive, but that an individual therapist could do better with problem solving (if needed, even on a temporary basis) and this resource was not wholly supplanted by the support group.

To get the names of support groups, start with churches, social agencies, and mental health centers. Almost all of these will have suggestions for you to follow up on, but they will likely not be able to give you details of the support groups as to number, membership, frequency of meetings, and the like. If you feel your support groups needs are very specific, then seek out support groups with such labels: Alcoholics Anonymous, stop-smoking groups, weight and diet control, and so forth. There are also support groups for people with problems with handicapped children, aging parents, and so forth, all of which groups can be located with a little bit of telephoning.

Unless you are pretty sure of your judgment, I would not recommend the costly and sometimes bombastic "support groups" such as est and the like. I am aware that some people swear by these costly, usually week-end programs, but some also sweat them, feeling their money was unwisely spent and that no new contribution was made to the person's welfare. Look carefully into any such commercial venture, partly by talking to friends or acquaintances who have gone; by talking with members of the staff of such commercial programs, and ask what are your consumer rights if you want to withdraw before the program ("retreat" or whatever it is called) is finished. Any money-back guarantees?

A useful reference on this point is the book-length study of the Encounter and Sensitivity movements of the 1960s, by Back (1971).[1] He feels that while the movement came about for many good reasons, such as social support, some excitement and entertainment, and because it got a lot of publicity, especially in its California setting, that it may have promised much more than it could deliver. Back entitles one chapter of his book, "Playing with Fire," in which it is pointed out that "During the conduct of encounter groups, people delve deeply into each other's lives, tell what they like and don't like about each other, and in general undermine each other's defenses. After this the person is supposed to go out and apply what he has discovered under the supposition that something he has learned in the group is true and correct" (p. 217).

Back points up one of the bugaboos often mentioned in this book, viz., the absence of good research backup for what one does in psychotherapy, which he alleges applies to the sensitivity and encounter movements. Some unsystematic evidence exists for people developing serious emotional problems, breakdowns, and/or hospitalization needs which appear to have been generated in the highly emotionally charged sensitivity and encounter group discussions (p. 219). There seems to have accumulated no evidence among the common run of support and self-help groups reaching such a high emotional pitch and risking serious emotional upset, although no one has good data on any of these kinds of ramifications among the rank and file of support groups, and not much evidence exists on this topic among students of psychotherapy[2] (see Chassick, 1971). The nature of the group leadership role in the sensitivity and encounter movement may make them more vulnerable to responsibility for emotional upset — identify the potential for them, handling them in the group, and being prepared to enlist alternative help — compared to the less formal support groups where roles and functions are less structured and responsibilities are presumably unclear and more personal toward friends and acquaintances. Back makes do two more points worth quoting: "It (the encounter and sensitivity movement) is a symptom of the new middle class, of the affluent society, and of the explosion of, and the search for, joy and new kinds of excitement" (p. 232); and in regard to change, — which is, of course, the object of all psychotherapy, support and other similar efforts, highly touted as the stated purpose of these more formal groups as well — Back says: ". . . change has been the commodity sold to clients by diverse organizations, and it is what the psych-resorts sell today" (p. 233). But change is presumably not just a transient affair, if it is seriously considered and pursued — it also implies a future effect. Whether these movements can promise in a bona fide way lasting change — and, also, whether they imply this kind of change — is something the consumers of these movements' offerings should check out very clearly. Given some of the problems apparently inherent in these larger scale, commercially extant sensitivity, encounter and support groups (by whatever names), the potential consumer of psychotherapy-like services should be wary and should make a strong effort to check out any given group and its promises. These commercial efforts may be presented in many guises: mountain retreats, singles' weekends (or week-long programs), trips, and so forth, some of them reaching (or reaching for) religious fervor along with your pocketbook.

WHO NEEDS MORE THAN SHORT-TERM PSYCHOTHERAPY HELP?

We have been quite critical in some ways concerning psychotherapy, and have stressed the greater economy — and about equal outcome results — found with the shorter varieties of therapy. Some readers may have gotten the impression that *all* psychotherapy should be short-term, and only that. There are important exceptions, not too well understood but seemingly legitimate cases of longer-term needs. Some people have the time and money to engage in longer-term therapy and, thereby, have the right to do so; it is mainly when insurance support for some places imbalance on the financial support of those more needy people who can get, use and pay for, only short-term help. Who are the legitimate longer-term cases?

In attempting to reply to that question, the reader should know that complete and firm answers are not available. Presumably psychotic persons need longer term help, at least in the form of social/educational/vocational monitoring, along with some drug support (if medically indicated), and/or support groups. They may not need intensive individual psychotherapy, however, as many of them began with such an effort and wound up in the hospital. Coming out of the hospital they need longer-term monitoring, as stated, so that they can become at least partially self-paying members of society rather than total charges on society.

Aside from these psychotic (or formerly psychotic) persons, who else needs longer-term help? Perhaps phobic and obsessive-compulsive cases do. They may begin psychotherapy, plus behavioral intervention programs, of a short duration and profit somewhat; when they do not profit clearly, they sometimes continue in longer-term intensive psychotherapy.[3] Although psychoanalytic psychotherapists seldom do empirical research, they state that the obsessive (and/or phobic) cases need prolonged help and represent cases in which sexual experiences are involved. The psychoanalytic viewpoint, then, puts the obsessive-compulsive cases and the phobic cases immediately in the category of long-term help. If people feel this is the case, irrespective of empirical evidence, then they may go into a "depth" therapy, either of the traditional type or some modification thereof. While behavioral methods have not been highly successful with these two sets of psychological disorders, neither has any other treatment.[4] It might be the wiser plan to begin with the more modest and up-front treatment — where the client knows in advance what is held to be important in explaining the difficulty and how the treatment will be conducted — so that possibilities for change are well-surveyed and engaged in before decisions are made to go the psychoanalytic route.

One therapeutic problem with obsessive and phobic cases — as well as with stopping smoking, stopping (excessive) caloric intake, and the like areas of behavior change — is that the emphasis has to be on *stopping* some complex and widely reinforced behaviors, rather than developing new behaviors from a low baseline. That is, if you are learning a new skill, chances are you start at the bottom level of that skill — say, throwing a boomerang — and do not have many competing responses to deal with. Building up from a low level is easier than cutting back from a high level of responsiveness. Obsessive and phobic cases have usually "practiced" their unwanted and disruptive behavior under wide circumstances for long periods of time, on intermittent schedules, hence these behaviors are strongly resistant to extinction (resistant to change or reduction). To control unwanted or objectionable behavior is harder than building up new behaviors, where the reinforcing circumstances are more available to the client and/or to environmental control. It will probably be a fairly long time before behavioral-experimental-clinicians gain the kinds of understanding and control necessary to make big changes in the behaviors of obsessive-compulsive and phobic clients. But then no other therapeutic viewpoint has offered much help, nor done any appreciable amount of research on the topics. Beech and Vaughan (1978) (see reference 4 above) are very straightforward in assessing the value of certain behavioral intervention procedures for tackling obsessive states, including self-control measures, systematic desensitization, modelling/flooding/response prevention, satiation training and thought stopping (pp. 165-169). These authors conclude:

> ". . . in the light of our review of treatment evidence, we must reluctantly conclude that there is no conclusive evidence that behavior modification offers a viable approach to the modification of abnormal thoughts in obsessionals (p. 169)."

And,

> Finally, we are in no doubt that much of the definitive work in this area remains to be done . . . in arriving at good answers to the question of the nature of obsessional mechanisms (p. 169).

However discouraging — or, perhaps, cautious is the better word — this may appear to one, there is a basic honesty in studying, assessing, and offering conclusions on this formidable area of study, an attitude not matched by the proponents of any other therapeutic viewpoint. Only with this kind of honesty, in preference to escaping a confrontation with what little we know about some areas of human behavior, will progress be made.

Other Considerations

Still other people will appear to require (or demand?) longer-term psychotherapy. We occasionally see students in the 18 to 30 year age range who come to the Counseling Center asking for referrals to longer-term therapists (our time limit is 10 sessions). Some of these had previous long-term therapy, running into the years in some instances, and they are asking for still more long-term help! It may be that long-term help begets long-term help, much of which thinking is promoted by the clinicians involved. These patients/clients seem to operate on the premise that "more is better." And, of course, these clinicians locate the basic cause of the person's difficulties "deep in the unconscious" which promotes a kind of mining expedition where no one knows exactly what is sought but the process is kept going anyhow. Moreover, no one would know when the patient and therapist had "gotten there," as no criteria other than behavior change — which is open to all viewpoints — is available to anyone, patient or therapist.

In one study done at The George Washington University Counseling Center on the relatively longer-term cases (fourteen sessions on the average, compared to the standard of about five sessions on the average, over a 1980-1984 baseline), we found no clear evidence as to why these cases went the longer period of time. They were not rated as more seriously disturbed by their therapists, in comparison to the standard time taken for comparable "control" cases seen by the same therapists, and they were not systematically referred out for more therapy at the time they left the Counseling Center treatment program. The only suggestive leads we could develop were related to the occurrence of what we called "extenuating circumstances" in the lives of these longer-running cases: The incidence of abortion, trouble with the law, failure in school, death or serious illness of a family member or a close friend. These incidents occurred somewhat more often among the extended cases than among the standard ones. We have to examine the problem much more than has been done; other clinics should look to this problem because of the relatively larger amount of time spent on the extended cases, to see how necessary is the extended time, and whether referral to a support group of persons with like experiences (e.g., death of a family member) would be preferable to continuance in individual therapy. This is one of the areas in which melding support group help with individual psychotherapy might prove very efficacious, a matter hardly ever studied systematically.

Some people feel that they and their problems require long, "deep" help, and thus they assume that that version of their difficulties is correct. They have not really challenged the notion by trying a good short-term therapist, hence they go on thinking as they had been taught. Community mental health clinics offer a good opportunity to study this problem as they have such a wide variety of clients that subgroups of very wide distribution as to seriousness, length of problems, and other considerations are available for study. In time, they will get around to this type of research and greatly improve their clinical acumen and skill in the doing. Right now we are not in a very good position to assess why some people need (or think they need) long-term help.

In my own clinical and psychotherapy experience, and among friends and acquaintances, I have (unsystematically) observed that those taking extra long times for their therapy have often had serious health and vocational problems in their lives or in the lives of close family members (especially spouses or children). They seem to move from one crisis to another, sometimes due to "bad luck," to faulty lifelong living habits, and to problems with others (who, themselves, need help) such as bosses and others in responsible or authorative positions vis-a-vis the patient. If I had all this to do over again, I would probably refer out these potentially long-term cases (although, admittedly, one does not know for sure who will turn out to be long-term) to support groups of careful choosing, to physicians for improved physical health care and health habits, and keep the therapy going on a "monitoring" basis, perhaps on a once-a-month, or like basis. These kinds of patients need long-term *care*, as I now see the matter, but not long-term psychotherapy in the problem-solving sense. Long-term therapy appears to inure some people to change, rather than promote change, and one has to be careful — and the profession must begin to develop more objective criteria than I, or anyone else, can possibly offer now — to note the difference between these two states of affair (long-term care versus psychotherapy). I say that presumably long-term care cases frequently need support rather than therapy, and this applies to group therapy as well; which, too often, only imitates long-term individual psychotherapy, purporting to do a more analytic and problem-solving job than it can likely do.

In final analysis, we know and understand very little about long-term psychotherapy, compared to what we know and can do in the short-term framework, hence it is a matter of extensive study which has only partly begun. Economically speaking, long-term therapy is very expensive; there should be some alternatives that are better all around: financially, human cost (and benefit) in time, energy, struggle, and final satisfaction.

Chapter 10

BEYOND THERAPY

THIS BOOK has tried to present a "level-headed" account of the present status of psychotherapy. In so doing, it has been important to tell the reader — whether therapist or client — that all is not well with psychotherapy *as it is usually presented to the consuming public.* While psychotherapy offerings certainly have redeeming values, much of what is touted is misleading, not backed up by research, and often misses the point of the real value to be found in psychotherapy.

In recent years several books have been published which have tried to give a more sober view of psychotherapy. Some review of these publications is in order.

Gross[1] (1978), wrote a book in which he purported to critically analyze psychiatry, psychotherapy, psychoanalysis and the so-called psychological revolution. He makes some interesting points (paraphrased here), paralleling what we have said earlier on in this book, to wit:

> "Human problems are not seen as normal variation or as the product of unusual circumstances, but as *internal psychological maladjustments*" (italics added) (p. 7) [All requiring, we might add, much therapy — my comments in brackets].
>
> "Most patients are female (62 percent), white (97 percent), and also middle-class, often diagnosed as "neurotic" (p. 22). [They have to be diagnosed somehow for statistical and insurance reimbursement.]
>
> "Originally the University of Chicago Counseling Center (in 1949) saw clients in psychotherapy for an average of 6 sessions" [this is comparable to the mean number of sessions I have identified in the psychotherapy literature, holding even for today], but by 1970, the average had increased to 45 sessions! (Gross, p. 31)." [Gross comes down hard on what he calls "psychonoxious" or unwanted, unsuccessful (even worsening) effects from psychotherapy] (Gross, p. 40), a term he coins which is similar to the legitimate term applied to physician influences of an adverse nature on patients, "iatrogenic," (literally, "physician caused"); and cites too much evidence to repeat

here for these untoward effects, one reference purporting to document psychotic breakdowns among Norwegian patients in intensive psychoanalytic psychotherapy (from Eysenck).[2]]

[Seemingly irrespective of sex, age, diagnosis, type of therapy, training of therapist, patient and therapist liking each other – Gross, p. 47, paraphrased – appeared to be a more solid basis for successful therapy.] [This finding is, of course, similar to those reported by Phillips (1985) across a wide collection of psychotherapy delivery systems.]

Therapists want "well people," ones not too disturbed, as "ideal" patients (Gross, p. 48). We have already alluded to the YAVIS syndrome: Young, Attractive, Verbal, Intelligent, and Stable persons, the preferred clients. In studies reported by Phillips (1985), it was shown that therapists and clients disagreed with each other on the clients' readiness for therapy (after intake) and the therapists' desire to work with specific clients they had interviewed . . . were they not enough YAVIS-like?]

[In a chapter (9, entitled, "The new therapies, the new messiahs," pp. 277-317), Gross is very hard on the new psychotherapies we have reviewed sparingly above, and somewhat more positively than Gross has. It is, however, very difficult to get excited about some of the newer therapies (e.g., Janou's Primal Scream therapy), inasmuch as they seem to repeat the main tenets of psychodynamic/psychoanalytic therapy with strong emphasis on abreaction and returning to the alleged origins of the individual's disturbances.]

Summarizing some of Gross' main points, the following can be said:

Neurosis is the malady of our age (p. 318). Millions of people are in psychotherapy at any one time, both in private and in community mental health settings (p. 318). It is a common mistake to confuse "neurosis" with unhappiness, although the latter is used to represent a state of affairs beyond simply absence of disease (*dis* ease) (p. 319). The main diagnostic criteria established by the American Psychiatric Association relies heavily on Freudian notions and these are located in the "psyche" for the most part (p. 320). All of us experience subjective distress – or overt distress – from which relief is sought in a variety of ways; does all this imply diagnosing one as "neurotic" and recommending extensive psychotherapy? (p. 320). People are not recommended to get support group, informal, grass roots help, for many of their problems, but are sent to the psychiatrist (sometimes, too, the psychologist or social worker, for *intensive* help). I can recall many cases of study skills/concentration deficits among university students who sought out – and often got – intensive psychiatric/psychoanalytic/psychodynamic therapy at the rate of 3 to 5 times a week for long periods, when they could have obtained more specific, behavioral help at the counseling center in from one to ten sessions (most likely 3 to 5 sessions!).

Gross' book raises a lot of imporant questions about psychotherapy. He has, however, taken as his model for criticism primarily Freudian psychoanalytic/psychodynamic types. He has no references for short-term therapy, does not address the so-called "dropout" (or, better, attrition) problem, and does not look at relationships between length of therapy and outcome, as judged by therapists and by patients. He does not systematically address issues related to client/therapist disagreements about therapy, especially about who is "workable" in therapy and how these differences affect the course of therapy. All of these points would have further substantiated some of his arguments about psychotherapy, but they would have also led him to more respect for short-term psychotherapy, a matter strongly addressed and emphasized in this book. His criticism mainly apply to the "depth" models for psychotherapy and he has marshalled good evidence for criticism of this kind of psychotherapy.

Even though therapists, qua therapists, may play somewhat on the gullibility of the client — aren't all consumers considered somewhat gullible by the marketers? — there are extant psychotherapy delivery systems which *are* practical, do their work in short periods of time, accept the fact that much of therapy is a matter of timely support and everyday practicalities, and pay some attention to how the client evaluates his/her therapy experiences. It is these latter types of short-term therapy, usually with a behavioral stance, that should draw some praise — even though some of these therapists still hold to the "depth" model and do not recognize or place up front their best images to the public. Gross seems to overlook these facts, or perhaps not even understand them.

We are not going to end therapy; it will be with us for a long, long time — until social living is greatly improved upon — so we should winnow down the important contributions it can make to peoples' living, cast off the surplus and unproductive stuff, and get on with a crisp, clear, effective short-term model.

Tennov[3] has written a more factual and sobering book on psychotherapy, albeit a critical one. Tennov points out that as an experimentally trained psychologist she had long held some reservations about the psychotherapy literature; additionally, she felt that psychotherapy was being aggressively promoted (without substantiating evidence for same), and as a woman she was appalled at the stories she heard in connection with the Women's Movement conference about women in psychotherapy and how they were treated. She feels that current behavioral practices have improved upon the kinds of therapy extant at the time she was a college student, and would wish for these improved therapy settings to be more typical of offerings today (pp. xi-xiii). Tennov also indicates how earlier efforts at publication were turned down because the publisher involved said [s/he] could not publish a book highly critical of psychotherapy due to the money made from books written by leading psychoanalysts (p. 13). This is a comment, then, not only on the state of the psychotherapy profession, but on the ways it has ramified into the commercial markets of publishers of books, with only sales as the issue.

Paraphrasing some of Tennov's writings the following appear important as useful contributions on the state of the psychotherapy profession.

Favored patients "[of the psychotherapists]" are not the "sickest" ones, [but those who meet a number of criteria, some of which are pretty personal on the part of the therapist, and they tend to stay in therapy] (Tennov, p. 15).

[The initial interview is stressed (Tennov, p. 21) and rightly so from the standpoint of research presented by Phillips (1985); but in the context on which Tennov reports, no mention is made of the loss of clientele at the first (intake) interview, and the gradual decline therefrom.]

[Research on psychotherapy of the Freudian variety is largely missing (Tennov, p. 73), and others' statements are confirmatory; some claiming psychoanalysis is not fully or really a therapy but a laboratory on which research on the psyche is done. However, the record shows little such research has been done or reported.]

[The generally lamentable state of research on psychoanalysis is well-covered (Tennov, pp. 74-77), plus evidence that these clinicians do not cooperate well with research and define the term much differently from the person who is experimentally and statistically trained in research.]

[Tennov, along with many others, quotes from Eysenck's work (Tennov, pp. 77-85), to the point that control groups of persons not undergoing therapy improve at about the same rate as those experiencing therapy. While this generalization by Eysenck has been highly disputed over the 30+ years since it was originally uttered, little evidence now exists that Eysenck was very wrong. The matter today is, however, the attrition curve, some of which evidence has been cited earlier in this book, a matter that complicates both Eysenck's work and that of his (more traditional) critics. If anything, the matter Eysenck spoke about has been complicated by the attritional phenomena, and bids the clinician and the patient be more careful in appraising psychotherapy efforts and findings.]

[On the possible "deterioration" effect from psychotherapy, and particularly with "depth" treatment, Tennov (pp. 89-100) is fairly clear and comprehensive, citing such matters as small number of cases in much of this research, evidence that some patients do become worse with treatment, interpretations of the patient's behavior that create more anxiety, a tendency to encourage dependency on the therapist, and some isolation from others occasioned with long-term treatment.]

[Anecdotal and selective evidence of help from psychotherapy is not hard to find (Tennov, pp. 104-106), but Tennov could have brought to bear a broader perspective on these pronouncements. Taking the selectivity into account, patients and therapists select one another more carefully than we often suppose, and we hear more about the successes than we do the failures or the so-so results. If short-term therapy is carefully compared to longer-term therapy, the former stands up as well as the latter and at considerably less cost, with a wider range of clientele and therapists (in Garfield, 1978).[4]

[Tennov is wise about and has respect for Carl Rogers and his research work on psychotherapy as well as his upending contributions to its scientific study (Tennov, pp. 163-168); while at the same time covering the opinions of others (mainly researchers) who have deplored the psychologist who turns attention to clinical work — sometimes with messianic fervor — away from experimentation and research, especially among the newer humanistic and existential varieties. In these cases of eschewing research it is hard to tell the psychologists from the psychiatrists and social workers, where neither of the last two named have much of a research tradition concerning psychotherapy.]

[In her final statement, Tennov (pp. 263-164) observes that results from psychotherapy are a mixed bag: some clients helped, some not, some perhaps harmed. More discouragingly for the profession — I should say the *professions* — of psychotherapy, it appears more likely that motivations are for economic gain. Tennov says: "Some psychotherapy professionals have given up the attempt to put their procedures on a scientific basis; perhaps their immediate concern is protecting their economic interests" (p. 263). Truly spoken words!]

[Consonant with many points made earlier in this book, Tennov raises questions about what will follow the psychodynamic/psychoanalytic model, and speculates that it may involve more self-help groups (as we have said above in this book); supportive roles among clinicians who know how to fit in with ongoing self-help programs; behavioral approaches; diet; exercise in the way of improved health regimens; and many informal groups, clubs, and associations (Tennov, pp. 263-264). While none of these is an end-all or be-all solution — and there should be no implication of a total solution — all of them may contribute somewhat more realistically and saliently to the needs of the general public for psychotherapy services. Most of Tennov's observations fit well with those espoused herein, even though many were written eight to ten years ago; if anything, her observations are more true and more urgent today than before.]

Dr. Bernie Zilbergeld has also written a high-flying book of criticism of psychotherapy services.[5]

What are some of the myths that Zilbergeld identifies and comments on? Some of these follow:

"The world is best understood in psychological terms" (p. 11). [Psychology extends to both the internal and external worlds. We generalize widely from psychology to economics, politics, religion, crime, physical illness, medicine, and so forth; some of which are fruitful, some unthinking generalizations. If anything goes wrong some say "psychologize it," or "get some treatment."]

"What you see is not necessarily what there is" (p. 14). [Most therapists — except behaviorists — assert that observable behavior is but the tip of the iceberg, to use the overworked cliche. Everything about behavior is caused beneath the surface, so to say, and the Freudian model is the hallmark of excellence and wisdom with this viewpoint. Trouble is, it has never been productive, as we have seen in this book.]

"People are not okay as they are" (p. 17). [The idea that every small psychological mishap is an occasion for a deep explanation, requiring treatment of the "depth" variety, is grossly overworked. People are seen to be less healthful, wise, creative, happy, and free than they may actually be. Pathology is personified. A mental health study of a sample of New Yorkers, 1950, found less than one-fifth rated as psychologically "well," a gross exaggeration if ever there was one. True, people can improve their lives, but for 4/5s to be pronounced "not well" is not in keeping with reality.]

"Individuals need to be liberated from the ties that bind" (p. 20). [People are characterized as having their creative natures distorted by repressive personal lives, occasioned by suppressive institutions such as religion and the church, family, sex roles and values, and society in general. The individual is the focus of psychotherapeutic change in these instances, even though the institution — which has never been well understood by psychology or any of the social sciences — may be partly to mostly to blame.]

"Everyone needs and can benefit from therapy" (p. 24). [All the world's a patient in this view. Is this because all people can benefit somewhat from self-knowledge — like increasing any other knowledge area — or is it that people *need* psychotherapy as the main or only route to self-knowledge and development? Taking the latter stand requires that we consult therapists and psychoanalysts, a conclusion for which there is no evidence (except for a small minority of persons).]

"The therapist is the expert and knows best" (p. 27). [Here is the arrogance of therapy and therapists operating at high speed, again.] Zilbergeld says "In practice, therapeutic freedom often means freedom from everything except the therapist's guidance" (p. 27). [This problem of the therapist's knowledge and role does not come forth at the start of therapy but when therapy is about to end] . . . the ". . . main battlegrounds between the wishes of the client and the supposedly greater knowledge of the therapist" (p. 28).

The popularity of psychotherapy cannot be gainsaid. Some statistics marshalled by Zilbergeld include the following paraphrased (p. 31): Encounter or sensitivity groups have drawn over five million people in the last fifteen years; TM (Transcendental Meditation) has drawn in about one million clients, similar to figures for marriage enrichment programs; the proliferation of nonprofessional programs for drugs, alcohol, and stopping smoking projects are uncountably great; and weight control programs also enroll millions a year.

Why do all of these psychotherapy-like programs proliferate? One reason is the perfectionistic motivations of the American people, probably unlike the motivations of most peoples from other nations. People laud the changes they allegedly receive from therapy and match stories with each other — like sports, fishing, and hunting stories — about their therapy, their therapist, and their successes. Zilbergeld recounts a conversation at a cocktail party (p. 3) where a woman insisted that therapy had changed her life; another guest said reading a mental health book had changed his life, and that several other books had had that influence on his life. Now all this fits into the area of relatively poor self-knowledge not only at the start of therapy but at its termination as well. Is it not like certain diets, a given play or movie, jogging, and a host of other things that presumably change lives? There is no differentiation here between entertainment, self-knowledge, small changes in one's outlook, and the correct utilization of modest but sometimes important sources of information. It is similar to the ads: "I *saved* $300.00 by going to Zilche's Chevrolet Agency."

One problem with these sweeping generalizations is that people are not really learning about themselves in substantive ways. I recall one 50 to 60 pound overweight woman who went to est and came back with the most glowing stories about its impact on her and how it helped her to lose 15-20 pounds, a matter she was continuing to work on. I saw her about three months later and she was her "same old self," with all the weight gained back and unwilling (she said) to go to est again and spend the hundreds of dollars for the temporary shot-in-the-arm it gave her.

How can all of these groups — est, encounter, and sensitivity groups, and many others — fit into the whole mental health/psychotherapy movement? How can genuine self-help and social support groups thrive at the modest level at which they are needed against the onslaughts and advertising of the "popular" groups which promise much and deliver little? One possible answer is reading books such as have just been exerpted in this chapter by Zilbergeld, Tennov, and Gross — and, of course, others — in order to get a more sober view of psychotherapy and what it and the support group movements can offer.

All peoples can improve their lives. No one has any quarrel with that generalization. But how? In what ways? At what cost? With what (lasting?) benefits? The psychotherapy market is just that — a market with now well over 250 varieties of psychotherapy (Herink, 1980),[6] all competing and trying to sell their wares in terms of the latest "gimmick" for changing behavior. Behavior can and does change, but in many cases change is very difficult, and it is difficult to maintain over time. There are just too many factors in peoples' lives that tend to stabilize their behaviors (good, bad or indifferent), whether they like it or not; and while psychotherapy of a *modest* sort might be welcome in many cases, it will have *modest* results.

People *are* interesting. Peoples' lives are interesting (not to mention perplexing, scandalous, unbelievable, admirable, nondescript); and so psychotherapists can engage people endlessly in these interesting discussions. But who is the benefactor? The patient? Somewhat, modestly. The therapist? Most likely, and most likely for financial reasons. It is not fair to condemn therapists — I have been one myself for 40 years — any more than it is to condemn physicians, lawyers, chief executive officers in large corporations, sales people who know not what they sell, as mercenary; but some of them are.[7] One has to judge the professions by their products. If therapy were so good, one or two would be outstanding and we'd all know it; as it is, the 250 varieties give no evidence of any substantive difference. Evidence for lasting benefits, research on outcomes, and willingness to have their theories and methods closely examined are mostly lacking.

WHAT DOES THE ACADEMIC COMMUNITY SAY ABOUT PSYCHOTHERAPY?

The books quoted above — and others that might be referred to — are of importance in asking people to take a closer look at their psychotherapy yearnings and try to evaluate more objectively what can be offered. These are good books, written by sincere and interested people, none of whom relies wholly on some theory of psychotherapy change and none of whom appears ulterior. But what about psychologists and physicians who study their professions as a whole and who have something to say not only to other psychologists (for whom they primarily write) but to the general public?

An experimental psychologist, Howard Kendler,[8] wrote an interesting book about psychology generally. Our interest here is in what Kendler says about areas related to our topic.

> Freudian theory falls short of this requirement [that is, that it cannot relate theory to observable fact] because it lacks any precision in its deductive capacity; any and all kinds of behavior appear consistent with it" (p. 154)

And

> Because their mode of functioning is not precisely stated, a Freudian theorist, with a modicum of ingenuity, has license to offer a consistent interpretation of any form of behavior occurring under any set of conditions" (p. 154).

Now the average person may not care whether Freudian psychotherapy is based on logical and empirically observable grounds, any more than one cares about the Consumer Reports on the car s/he is driving, the nicotine content in the cigarettes smoked or the "therapy results" of an est encounter program. But the evaluator of psychotherapy programs does care about these matters — this book cares about these matters — and in the long run the average consumer will benefit by this kind of criticism.

The practical point for the psychotherapy consumer arising from the Kendler quotes is that one cannot trust the psychoanalytic movement, in the form of its psychotherapy, to be responsible for its methods, its theory or its practice. If "anything goes" is the motto, where is the reliability in it all? In the study of science as method — called the philosophy of science — one has to have propositions, hypotheses, theories, etc. that are testable, that can be confirmed or shown to be wrong: falsifiable. If, for example, we believed that all women as a group drove cars more recklessly than men, had to pay higher insurance premiums and take more severe licensing exams, that would be a belief (or hypothesis, or proposition) that could be tested and shown to be wrong (falsifiable). To then show it was false would be a boon to women, not to mention fairness to men and to society generally, as well. It is important that our beliefs and rules and theories and what-not, that we follow — in psychotherapy as well as in other practical affairs — be subject to scientific test and scrutiny. Psychoanalysis/psychodynamic psychotherapy does not meet these criteria. Short-term therapy, on the other hand, has not been tested in all of its varieties; the best we can say now is that its propositions are more readily testable (can it show equally good results in shorter time and for less cost?). A proposition then that states that short-term therapy, for most people most of the time, is equal to or better than Freudian therapy (in terms of agreed upon outcome findings), can be tested, it can be rendered false. That is enough to set up a short-term therapy as more closely approximate to scientific criteria — hence, in time, or perhaps already, of greater practical value to the consuming public.

When psychologists write for each other in their journals and books, they are sometimes more candid than when they write for the public. Many of these writing for the former seldom write for the general public. Looking into the more technical writing, then, can offer perspective not easily present to the average consumer of psychotherapy services.

For example Garfield and Kurz[9] report on their research on a group of patients offered (and they accepted) treatment in an outpatient clinic. The average number of sessions was about 6 sessions, and very few went more than 10 interviews, and very, very few more than 25 interviews; although this report was not based on a time-limited or short-term context. Moreover, 57.5 percent of the cases had less than 5 interviews. This finding could be repeated almost endlessly from clinics treating alcoholic patients, university counseling centers treating people with an average age of about 22 to 23 years, community mental hygiene and health centers throughout the whole of the USA, and so forth (see Phillips, 1985 for a more detailed review of these findings).[10] These are sobering figures; psychotherapy is not, in the general scheme of things, or in the public sector, a long-term, expensive, arduous matter; it is much different from the *New Yorker* cartoon stereotype of psychotherapy as a "couch job" that takes years and years.

In spite of these short-term treatment facts, Garfield and other psychologists speak of people "dropping out of therapy" (as if this were a "bad" thing, as if it meant that help was not forthcoming, as if it meant that such cases were necessarily "failures"), and do not take fully into consideration that the average modal treatment figures for the entire country, irrespective of diagnosis, mode of treatment, training of the therapists and theoretical persuasions, is about 4 to 8 sessions (as had been stated, above, in other contexts).

One would think that therapists, themselves, would study, account for, and report much more in psychotherapy research than they do. In reviewing the research on "therapist variables," that is, the characteristics of therapists, their training, and so forth, that are expected to influence client success and outcome, Parloff et al. have this to say:[11]

> The therapist variables most frequently selected by the researchers for study are, unfortunately, such simplistic, global concepts as to cause this field to suffer from possible terminal vagueness. Therapist variables categorized as personality, mental health, experience, sex, race socioeconomic status, and so on, can be usefully related to specific treatment goals only at a gross probabilistic level. The actual therapeutic mechanisms that may be embedded in these molar concepts remain obscure.

So what does this mean, Mr. and Mrs. consumer of psychotherapy? It probably means that you can choose your therapist — assuming they are qualified, licensed, and otherwise appropriate (fees, for example) — as well as anybody else. No great margin of superiority resides in anyone, and the final matter is up to you. You do not need a Freudian analyst, a Rogerian nondirective therapist, a no-nonsense behaviorist (unless you know you do on personal grounds); you need someone you can feel confident in, relate to, who treats you with respect and concern, and who is not trying to keep you in therapy for the sake of the matter, or imposing a lot of serious problems *on you* in order to promote more therapy.

We have given several indications in this book that therapists have a number of "demands" they place on clients/patients. One is to come back for therapy after the intake interview. Failure to return to therapy after the intake characterized about 45 to 55 percent of a university clientele, over a 4-year period of time (Phillips, 1985). Therapists often feel rejected by the clients who fail to return, who "fail," in effect, to take up the kind and considerate and empathic offer of the therapist to continue with therapy. However, the prevalence of clients not taking up on this offer is demonstrable. But when these people (who choose not to return after intake) are called concerning their visit to the clinic, about two-thirds to 70 percent (or higher) report "satisfaction," that is, they do not feel rejected by the clinic or the therapist, do not themselves reject the offer for negative reasons, and often say they did not return because of practical issues in their lives (Bloom p. 172).[12] Bloom's comment about these and similar findings in a variety of clinics seems highly pertinent to this book and to the present discussion: "Therapists consistently underestimated the help which clients with unplanned closings judged they had received, and they consistently overestimated how helpful they had been to clients with planned closings" (p. 172). Essentially, then, therapists are supposed to have charge; it is not "cricket," per the therapists' opinions, for the client to take matters in his/her own hands and terminate "prematurely." With this kind of attitude among therapists — prevailing as it often does, especially among "depth" therapists — it is no wonder that there are strong prejudices for and against psychotherapy.

The middle ground of a practical, client-oriented, behavior change procedure is not as conceptually clear among therapists as it might be, and not as well brought forward for public scrutiny as it might be.

Recently research psychologists, some of whom are also clinicians, have made a more systematic effort to study the outcomes from psychotherapy.[13] They have studied widely different populations of children, adolescents, young adults, high school and college students, adults with a variety of diagnoses treated by a variety of psychotherapy methods. These findings have been combined in various statistical ways in order to study whether psychotherapy, en masse, does produce a beneficial effect, and whether different psychotherapies have it much over one another. The results of such analyses on several hundred research reports and based on about 1,400 measures of change associated with psychotherapy show mixed results.

Various symposia and a number of replies to the Smith et al. research have been published. One such brief comment is by Gallo (1978), based on an earlier report by Smith and Glass (along the same lines as the 1980 book, however), summarizes the findings that most clearly apply to our discussion here: "Given the reanalysis of the data that I have presented, the appropriate conclusions are as follows: (a) Psychotherapy has a real, measurable, and quite weak effect upon the dependent measures [they are the approximately 1,400 measures used, cited above, to evaluate psychotherapy outcome], and (b) different types of psychotherapy have a real, measurable, and quite weak effect upon the adjustment scores that constitute the dependent measures, and this effect becomes even weaker when therapy types are aggregated into superclasses and relevant variables are equated.[14]

Gallo's conclusion, after reworking some of the original data, is essentially what we are holding to in this book. It may be that the more practical of the many, many varieties of therapy — perhaps most likely various behavioral interventions — are associated with economies and practicalities, given the whole enterprise of delivering psychotherapy to the public. In-the-office therapies probably do not stand up as much different from each other unless they attempt to be short-term, practical, and economical in matters of payment, training of therapists, and so forth.

One small demur: Even though we speak and write about behavior therapists, psychoanalytic therapists, Gestalt therapists, and so on, we should not assume that all of these within a given persuasion are equally good or even do the "same" thing. There must be the same variety among therapists of each and every persuasion that there are between persuasions (or nearly so), and if true that would make generalizations about therapy outcome from any one or more therapy persuasions moot. In time, researchers will be better prepared to study the in-therapy actions of therapists more accurately and assiduously, which will give us a better leg up on this problem and help to separate out the therapeutic behaviors of "good" and "bad" therapists of each persuasion. Right now, however, we have to fly a lot by the seats of our pants when choosing a therapist; and his/her persuasion, with a few exceptions, will apparently not make a great deal of difference.

Chapter 11

ADDENDUM

IN READING over the chapters in this book, some colleagues of mine suggested that I attempt to clinically pin down many of the observations and strictures cited; that is, relate the overall short-term emphasis to the actual clinical situation, to the actual exchange between therapist and client. The following topics arise directly from interactions with clients; they are also topics much discussed with my graduate students in a psychotherapy seminar, in which their tapes and mine have been played and discussed; now for some 23 years.

Each of the following points would, ideally, take a chapter in a book, with illustrations from actual therapy protocols (recorded); however, that much detail is unnecessary in this briefer context. The reader is invited to try out the following topics in his/her therapy, and/or with his/her patients. The more one tries to apply these points, the more they seem salient.

1. Clients will tell you (the therapist) their problems early on in the therapy, as early as the first few minutes! These "tellings" will not arise in clear, crisp, conceptually relevant ways, but yet specific enough that you as therapist — or you, alternatively, as client — can discern them. They may, then, become priorities in the therapy; they usually call for much more discussion, and for later confirmation or disconfirmation.
2. The therapist should not sit there and think to him/her self something considerably different about the client than the client is revealing or discussing. Two channels of communication are not better than one; one is enough. Say, Mr. or Mrs. Therapist, what you are thinking . . . but in acceptable language; do not spend your time "thinking diagnosis" about the client, but concentrate as pointedly as possible on what the client is saying or doing, and respond accordingly.
3. Following from 2, you as therapist, and as client, each, has the right to say what you want to say; establish that agreement at the outset. We have always taught clients to feel free to say anything they wanted to

say — even about the therapist — and the same rule and fairness applies to the therapist. Each has this inalienable therapeutic right. The sayings, however, should preferably not be in abrasive language but can more readily be understood and accepted if they are stated in such a way as the following: "It seems to me you are doing . . . or feeling . . . or saying . . .; and I wonder if I am right?" The candidness should be honest, salient, nonaccusatory, but straightforward.

4. The client's failure to see or to take alternative action is not due to "repression" of feeling and the like, but to not knowing or accepting or trusting the alternatives. As soon as a client can see, understand, and concretely work on alternatives to his/her problems, the client can move to testing them out and, then, to accepting them, or not; or moving on to other alternatives. What we often call "defense" or "unconscious" workings, and the like, are simply the result of failure to get with alternatives. It is not due to some "blocking" — like a boulder in the road — of client responsiveness, however appealing that metaphor might appear to some.
5. The client need not accept the therapist's "diagnosis" and there should be very little time spent on diagnosis, as such (save for administrative or insurance reimbursement purposes); and the therapist should not concentrate on diagnosis. Both parties (or all parties, if we are in a goup setting) should concentrate on the behavior, its antecedents, and its consequences; there is plenty of subject matter in this kind of analysis to keep people busy with the change enterprise.
6. The beginning of therapy is probably much more important than the ending. While both, in a way, need to be prepared for — ideally — the client and therapist have more time to prepare for the ending. In most traditional thinking the ending is greatly embellished in its importance, as if it were the parting of the century. This is an unwise emphasis if the ending is fairly well-stated at the outset, and agreed upon (or altered, with mutual consent), and so the tapering off is a matter of course. There is no "transference" to overcome; rapport, a much more honest and relevant term, is simply a goodwill loosening of the relationship. If the client has plans, new or altered goals, and the like, that is something to look forward to, to get on with, to be challenged by. The greatly embellished ending of traditional therapy is more of a selfish matter on the part of the therapist and should not be given great importance by wise therapists or clients. Thinning out the last few interviews in short-term (or time-limited) therapy is often a good way to end; taking, say, the last three interviews in a 10-session framework on the basis of a two- or three-week interval rather than the usual one-time-a-week plan.
7. It is important for the therapist to recognize that the client may refuse to talk about some subjects. This is a right that must be acknowledged and

respected. More traditional "depth" therapists would say what one chooses not to talk about, or refuses to mention and discuss is, perforce, of vast importance. I doubt this altogether. This viewpoint on the therapist's part represents a clash in theories about therapy, what therapy is in its larger sense, how the therapy sessions should be conducted and to what ends. One point against the dire view of "client resistance," one must remember, is that client's later talk about originally suppressed (suppressed, not repressed) topics and feeling is that they have to get the matter better in hand before disclosing much, and also to see how alternatives to their guarded information may be worked out. The client requires respect for his/her views in this matter; looking down the (therapist's) nose at the client in a superior manner will not the problem remedy. If the therapist yields to the client's preference in not discussing some topics, this allows their interactions to be kept on a more productive basis, avoiding a one-upmanship attitude on the therapist's part. Also, one must note that discussing every topic is not, perforce, needed for gainful therapy to take place; most therapy can be productive when only a few topics are handled.

8. Although we often describe our own behavior and that of others as "unreasonable," "bizarre," "unspeakable," etc., whatever behavior occurs in a given situation is, of necessity, appropriate in relation to the person and the situation s/he feels caught up in. The *outcome,* the consequences, may be all of the "horrible" things, but the behavior, as such, is as natural as breathing. One gains better control over one's behavior — and the therapist's help in this process is more optimal — when the unwanted behavior (or, for that matter, sporadic behavior that is desired but is not always forthcoming, such as might be represented by acceptable social performances or task-relevant behavior) is viewed as a natural result of natural circumstances. While the client would not be in therapy if change were not desired, it does not help matters to give unwanted behavior negative and moralistic and condemnatory names at the outset; the unwantedness of the behavior is already apparent, and what is needed for correction is better understanding and control over the antecedent conditions (and later reinforcement) that help bring about and maintain the unwanted behavior.
9. Client and therapist (urgently) meeting over the critical issues takes some judgment. This observation is different from a crisis where a person is about to do harm to himself (herself) or another. It is, rather, a situation in which the client is behaving very impulsively (some would say "hysterically") in response to a situation. Basically, the client is having a kind of subdued temper tantrum, showing considerable anger, reactive depression of a momentary nature, or the like. One patient came in, sat down in a kind of "huff," and said, "Well, you're lucky I'm here today!"

Why *I* was lucky, I don't know, but anyhow that was her tact. She was angry about having trouble finding a parking space (for the second time that day, both unrelated to the therapy session, as she had a dental appointment prior to the therapy session), and said she was just about ready to "give up on me" (meaning the therapist). Some discussion showed she was angry from a spat with her husband earlier in the day, then the two parking problems followed. Another young man said he was "so depressed he could not go on any longer . . ." owing to having been turned down by a girlfriend of recent origin. Therapy conducted with these seemingly critical situations calls for lots of patience and an effort to get past the immediate provocations and onto firmer ground.

10. Clients are advised to think of their problems as basically conflict situations, usually conflicts between what they want (desire, feel they need, aspire to . . .) and what is forthcoming. Problems are problems if there are discrepancies between what is actually the case and what one wishes – maybe demands – it to be. If this formulation is well-understood, the therapist can always call upon the client to "Say what the conflict . . . is about" and often thereby help clear up matters and lead into better understanding and self-control.
11. Although we have said above that the client tells the discerning therapist early on what his/her problem is, in the absence of the therapist pointing this out and working some on it, the client may appear aimless, wandering, confused, self-contradictory, and the like at the start of therapy (if this obtains later on, both therapist and client should look more carefully into the matter of how therapy is progressing). It is typical in the therapeutic literature to say that clients are greatly confused, ambivalent, and the like early on. One way to help ameliorate this condition and to move toward greater clarity is to divide the client's problems into various areas: work, home, wife, children, peers, and so forth. Or, particular emotional reactions such as anger, reactive depression, etc. may be the discernibly recurrent characteristic to work on. As the subsequent hours occur, after naming some such problem areas, they can begin with a review of the major problem area and an up-date made. This keeps both therapist and client clearly in touch with each other about substantive issues, helps identify what is needed for further progress, sets tasks for between-therapy-session activities, and also sets an agenda for subsequent meetings.
12. As a generalization that includes many, many details, one important overarching matter in therapy is to *keep structure*. That is a matter of therapist responsibility at the outset; later on, both therapist and client can hold to this responsibility. Keeping structure is meant to cover topics that are agreed upon and worked on; ways of handling problems and reporting back on them; changing tactics if some are not working well;

deciding upon a change of emphasis if new problems have arisen in the client's life; evaluating all of these considerations; and generally keeping on top of things.

13. Both client and therapist should regard the other as an ally. It may not always be the case, but it is the best starting position to take; if it proves incorrect, one will know it sooner if it is explicitly made open at the outset than if one meanders about the problem for weeks or months before acknowledging that the alliance is missing. I have talked with many patients/clients who have said of previous therapy experience that they didn't like the therapist (but were too timid to mention it, or to seek other help, for fear of looking bad in their own or someone's eyes), and that they think they never could have had a gainful relationship with *that* therapist. This is understandable: not all of us like all other people, therapist, client, or just ordinary relationships, and we should not be expected to have this regard across the board. However, if it is evident that a lack of rapport is present, some actions should be taken about it as soon as possible and not let it be considered as some kind of deep-going "resistance" that has to be "worked through" over large spans of time.
14. The most discernible help will likely come early on in therapy. This does not necessarily mean that all problems will be solved with dispatch, but that the embryo of change, so to speak, will be laid down early. Even in long-term therapy, patients have stated that they felt the most discernible changes took place relatively early — within three to six months — and later therapy was mostly polishing up the changes. One has the right, of course, to elect to do this "polishing" but it is not required for therapeutic change, and one should know that the choice is open to him/her (both therapist and client should openly acknowledge this strong possibility about early on change).
15. There is nothing wrong with both client and therapist agreeing, at the point of termination (or in discussing its possibility beforehand) that the client can return for a "refresher" later on. We encounter this commonly in the university setting, where a client (say) has had only 3-4 sessions before a summer vacation and wants to come back in the fall — or hold open this possiblity — with the advent of the new school year, without any interim, help. Therapists and the clinic policy that regulate much of the delivery of services should keep open these kinds of arrangements. Several clients I have had in the university setting have wanted to take some "time off" for a variety of reasons, then return for a few interviews later, and we have always tried to accommodate these requests. Therapy should not be regarded as some formidable affair that cannot tolerate interruptions; it should be as flexible as the shared demands between therapist and client make possible.

16. The sharing of information or the therapist's willingness to see another member of the client's family (husband or wife, commonly) should also be viewed flexible. One does not see the spouse against the client's will, of course; but often an interview or two with another family member can be very illuminating in behalf of the principle client's objectives; provided, of course, it is all agreed upon openly and is not construed as have some underhanded objectives such as checking-out-the-client-to-see-if-he/she's-telling-the-truth. Often enough the client will ask the therapist to see the spouse (adolescents are not as gracious about parents being interviewed, however) so that a number of matters can be seen more directly by the therapist. However the mutual agreement falls, this should be the respected basis for judging what to do in relation to the client's welfare.
17. Can phone calls substitute for in-office interviews now and then? In the interest of flexibility and meeting exigencies in the client's life, yes. If they get out of hand and represent some other motivation — such as a client being reluctant to say s/he wants to stop and is unable to bring the matter up forthrightly — the use of phone calls has naturally to be brought up in the regular therapy context and reevaluated. When writing therapy was originally used by some psychoanalysts it came about because each, client and therapist, saw the need to stay in touch, but with illness, vacations, and the like making this impossible, mail contact sufficed for a while. Telephone calls can serve the same interim purpose; not as a total substitute for the face-to-face meetings, but as a functional adaptation to meet unusual, but temporary, situations. If calls are used to fade out, then this should be as up-front as, indeed, all therapeutic interactions should; and dealt with accordingly.
18. The same can be said for using writing as a substitute for in-office contacts, unless the writing has been agreed upon as a total process quite apart from face-to-face meetings. Sometimes the candidness of both phone calls and/or writing, in lieu of face-to-face meetings, has to be given preference, but also has to be looked at anew (if the main therapy began as a face-to-face matter) because it may signal a change on the client's part that needs open consideration.
19. An important consideration in therapy is to recognize that problems do not necessarily stem from their opposite. Clinicans often assume that if a person is "super nice," he/she assumes the person is really feeling very hostile and is masking the hostility by its opposite, being very cordial. This practice assigns characteristics and motivation to people that may not be true. It overlooks the possibility that the super nice person has been reinforced for this behavior and that is all it represents. In the interest of parsimony, one should take the behavior first at its face value, dealing as well as possible with it, then go on to other possibilities, if the

first one proves unproductive. Too much time is wasted in therapy tortuously seeking out alleged origins in meanings when there simply isn't anything there. This can make long-term therapy out of simpler short-term efforts.

20. The assumption is frequently made that behavior that occurs in the therapy hour must also of necessity occur on the outside. Occasionally clinicians assume that if outside behavior of significance does not occur in therapy, that the client is "repressing" this behavior or perhaps not acting honestly in reporting on him/her self. In a typical therapy interaction anger, for one thing, may not occur; sexually-related behavior may not occur; behavior related to many kinds of social skills may have no relevance, hence, may not occur, and so forth. If behavior relevant outside does occur, or can be elicited, then that certainly becomes subject matter for therapy. It is economical then to deal with those behaviors as such. This is far from assuming that there is some integral relationship that occurs of necessity between the out-of-therapy and in-therapy behavior of the client. If the connection is there, in short, then use it; if not, do not go on a witch hunt.

Others engaging in short-term psychotherapy may have similar observations to make regarding the conduct of therapy. One should attempt to see these kinds of attitudes broadly, not as eternal truths, but as working arrangements between therapist and client that can lead to an effective and efficient relationship. Any matters that come before client and therapist should contribute to those objectives in whatever ways that benefit the client.

REFERENCES AND NOTES

Introduction

1. *Provisional Data on Federally Funded Community Mental Health Centers,* 1978-1979. Rockville, Md.: National Institute of Mental Health, 1981.
2. Phillips, E.L. and Johnston, M.H.S. Theory and Development of Short-Term, Parent-Child Psychotherapy, *Psychiatry,* 1954, 17, 267-275.
3. Eysenck, H.J. The Effects of Psychotherapy: An Evaluation. *Journal of Consulting Psychiatry,* 1952, 16, 319-324.
4. Phillips, E.L. and Wiener, D.N. *Discipline, Achievement and Mental Health.* Inglewood Cliffs, New Jersey: Prentice-Hall, 1962. (2nd Edit.)
5. Phillips, E.L. *Psychotherapy: A Modern Theory and Practice.* Inglewood Cliffs, New Jersey: Prentice-Hall, 1956.
6. Phillips, E.L. *Counseling and Psychotherapy: A Behavioral Approach.* New York: Wiley, 1977.

Chapter 1
What Have Others Said of Short-Term Psychotherapy?

1. Budman, S.H. (Editor)., *Forms of Brief Therapy.* New York: Guilford, 1981.
2. Rogers, C.R. and Dymond R., *Psychotherapy and Personality Change.* Chicago: University of Chicago Press, 1954.
3. See Reference 2, Introduction.
4. Phillips, E.L., *Love, Poetry and Psychotherapy.* New York: Irvington, 1985. (In Press)
5. Frank, J.D. et al., Patient's Expectancies and Relearning as Factors Determining Improvement In Psychotherapy. *American Journal of Psychiatry,* 1959, 115, 961-968.
6. Wells, R.A., *Planned Short-Term Treatment.* New York: Free Press, 1982.
7. Budman, S.H., See Reference 1, above.
8. Sifneos, P.E., Short-Term Anxiety-Provoking Psychotherapy: an Emotional, Problem-Solving Technique, *Seminars in Psychiatry,* I., 4 (November, 1969). Sifneos, P.E., *Short-Term Dynamic Psychotherapy: Evaluation and Technique.* New York: Plenum Press, 1979.
9. Malan, D.H., *A Study of Brief Psychotherapy.* New York: Plenum Press, 1963.
10. Wilson, G.T., Behavior Therapy as a Short-Term Therapeutic Approach. In Budman, See Reference 1, above.
11. Alexander, F. and French, T.M. *Psychoanalytic Therapy: Principles and Applications.* New York: Ronald Press, 1946.
12. Bloom, B.L., Focused Single Session Therapy: Initial Development and Evaluation. In Budman, S.H., See Reference 1, above.
13. Wilson, G.T., See Reference 10, above. See also, Phillips and Wiener, Reference 4 in Introduction.
14. Ewing, C.P. *Crisis Intervention as Psychotherapy.* New York: Oxford University Press, 1978.

15. Budman, S.H., See Reference 1, above. Goldring, J. *Quick Response Therapy: A Time-Limited Treatment Approach.* New York: Human Sciences Press, 1980.
16. Berman, P.J., David, A.W. and Phillips, E.L., George Washington University Volunteer Hotline, A Descriptive Study, *Psychological Reports,* 1973, 33, 364-366.
17. Ewing, C.P. See Reference 14, above.
18. Borman, D.L., et al., *Helping People to Help Themselves: Self Help and Prevention.* New York: Haworth, 1982. Royce, J.R. and Mos, L.P. (Editors). *Humanistic Psychology, Concepts and Criticisms.* New York: Plenum, 1981. Maguire, L., *Understanding Social Networks.* Beverly Hills: Sage Publications, 1983. Stokes, B., *Helping Ourselves: Local Solutions to Global Problems.* New York: W.W. Norton, 1981.
19. Ewing, C.P. See Reference 14, above.
20. Ewing, C.P. See Reference 14, above.
21. Berman, P.J., et al. See Reference 16, above.
22. Parad, H.J. and Parad, L.G. A Study of Crisis-Oriented Planned Short-Term Treatment: Part One. *Social Case Work,* 1968, 49, 346-355.
23. Parad, H.J. and Parad, L.G. See Reference 22, above. Shaw, R., et al. A Short-Term Treatment Program in a Child Guidance Clinic, *Social Work,* 1968. 13, 81-90.
24. Donovan, J.M., et al. The Crisis Group: Its Rationale, Format and Outcome. In Budman, S.H. See Reference 1, above.
25. Langsley, D.G., et al. Family Crisis Therapy: Results and Implications, *Family Processes,* 1968, 7, 145-158.

Chapter 2
Why Do People Seek Psychotherapy?

1. Zilbergeld, B. *The Shrinking of America: Myths of Psychological Change.* Boston: Little, Brown & Co., 1983.
2. Bloom, B.L. In Budman, S.H. See Reference 12, Chapter 1.
3/4. Phillips, E.L. *The Social Skills Basis of Psychopathology: Alternatives to Abnormal Psychology and Psychiatry.* New York: Grune & Stratton, 1978.
5. Phillips, E.L. *Psychotherapy: A Modern Theory and Practice.* Englewood Cliffs, New Jersey: Prentice-Hall, 1956.

Chapter 3
The Main Theories of Psychotherapy: I. Psychodynamic and Behavioral

1. Zilbergeld, B., See Reference 1, Chapter 2.
2. Budman, S.H., See Reference 1, Chapter 1.
3. Strupp, H.H., Toward the Refinement of Time-Limited Dynamic Psychotherapy. In Budman, S.H., See Reference 1, Chapter 1.
4. Hollingshead, A.B., and Redlich, F.C., *Social Class and Mental Illness.* New York: Wiley, 1958.
5. Phillips, E.L., *Psychotherapy Revised: New Frontiers in Research and Practice.* Hillsdale, New Jersey: Erlbaum, 1985 (In Press).
6. Fagan, P.J., The Fagan Study of Intake. In Phillips, E.L., See Reference 5, above.
7. Tennov, D., *Psychotherapy: The Hazardous Cure.* New York: Anchor Books, 1976.
8. Garfield, S.L., Research on Client Variables in Psychotherapy. In S.L. Garfield and A.E. Bergin (Editors), *Handbook of Psychotherapy and Behavior Change: An Empirical Analysis* (2nd Ed.) New York: Wiley, 1978.

9. Tennov, D., See Reference 7, above.
10. Tennov, D., See Reference 7, above, especially pages 92-100.
11. Tennov, D., See Reference 7, above, especially pages 210-247.
12. Tennov, D., See Reference 7, above. Phillips, E.L., *Stress, Health and Psychological Problems in the Major Professions.* Lanham, Maryland: University Press of America, 1982.
13. Kalish, H.I., *From Behavioral Science to Behavior Modification.* New York: McGraw-Hill, 1981. Krasner, L., Behavior Therapy, *Annual Rev. of Psychology,* 1971, 22, 483-532. Kazdin, A.E., *A History of Behavior Modification: Experimental Foundations of Contemporary Research.* Baltimore: University Park Press, 1978.
14. Haring, N.G. and Phillips, E.L., *Analysis and Modification of Classroom Behavior.* Inglewood Cliffs, New Jersey: Prentice-Hall, 1972. Martin, G. and Pear, J., *Behavior Modification: What It Is and How To Do It.* Inglewood Cliffs, New Jersey: Prentice-Hall, 1982. Rimm, D.C. and Masters, J.C., *Behavior Therapy: Techniques and Emperical Findings.* New York: Academic Press, 1979.
15. Eysenck, H.J., *Handbook of Abnormal Psychology.* London: Pitman, 1960.
16. Eysenck, H.J., See Reference 3, Introduction.
17. Wolpe, J., *Psychotherapy by a Reciprocal Inhibition.* Stanford: Stanford University Press, 1958.
18. Strupp, H.H. and Hadley, S.W., A Tripartite Model of Mental Health and Therapeutic Outcomes: With Special Reference to Negative Effects in Psychotherapy, *American Psychologist,* 1977, 32, 187-196.
19. Tennov, D., See Reference 7, above.
20. Singleton, W.T., et al., *The Analysis of Social Skill.* New York: Plenum, 1980.
21. Phillips, E.L., See Reference 3, Chapter 2.
22. Beck, A.T., Cognitive Therapy: Nature and Relation to Behavior Therapy, *Behavior Therapy,* 1970, 1, 184-200. Mahoney, M.J. *Cognitive and Behavior Modification.* Cambridge, Mass: Ballinger, 1974. Meichembaum, D. *Cognitive-Behavior Modification: An Integrative Approach.* New York: Plenum, 1977.
23. Phillips, E.L., See Reference 5, above.
24. Budman, S.H., See Reference 1, Chapter 1.
25. Budman, S.H., See Reference 1, Chapter 1. Sifneos, P.E., Short-Term Anxiety-Provoking Psychotherapy: Its History, Technique, Outcome and Instruction, in Budman, S.H., See Reference 1, Chapter 1. Gustafson, J.P., The Complex Secret of Brief Psychotherapy in the Works of Malan and Balint, in Budman, S.H., See Reference 1, Chapter 1.
26. Gustafson, J.P., See Reference 25, above.
27. Kalish, H.I., See Reference 13, above. Bachrach, A.J., Erwin, W.J., & Mohr, J.P., The Control of Eating Behavior in an Anorexic by Operant Conditioning Techniques. In L.P. Ullmann and L. Krasner, (Eds.), *Case Studies in Behavior Modification.* New York: Holt, Rinehart & Winston, 1965.

Chapter 4
The Main Theories of Psychotherapy: II. Rogerian, Humanistic, Rational-Emotive Therapies and Beck on Depression

1. Rogers, C.R. *Counseling and Psychotherapy.* Cambridge, Mass: Houghton Mifflin, 1942. Rogers, C.R. The Necessary and Sufficient Conditions of Psychotherapeutic Personality Change, *Journal of Consulting Psychologists,* 1957, 21, 95-103. Rogers, C.R. *Client-Centered Therapy: Its Current Practices, Implications, and Theory.* (Second Edition). Boston: Houghton Mifflin, 1965.

2. Maslow, A.H. *Motivation and Personality.* New York: Harper & Row, 1954. Lowry, R.J. *The Journals of Abraham Maslow.* Lexington, Mass: Lewis Publishing Co., 1982.
3. Lambert, M.J., Introduction to Assessment of Psychotherapy Outcome: Historical Perspective and Current Issues, in M.J. Lambert, et al., *The Assessment of Psychotherapy Outcome.* New York, Wiley, 1983.
4. Sears, R.R. Experimental Analyses of Psycho-Analytical Phenomena in J. McV. Hunt (Editor), *Fundamentals of Personality and Behavior Disorders.* New York: Ronald Press, 1943.
5. Corsini, R.J. *Handbook of Innovative Psychotherapies* (Editor). New York: Wiley, 1981.
6. Bindrim, P. Aqua-Energetics, in Corsini, R.J. See Reference 5, above.
7. Losoncy, L. Encouragement Therapy, in Corsini, R.J. See Reference 5, above.
8. Dreikurs, R. *Psychology in the Classroom.* New York: Harper & Row, 1968.
9. Combs, A.W., Richards, A.C., and Richards, F. *Perceptual Psychology: A Humanistic Approach to the Study of Persons.* New York: Harper & Row, 1976. Snygg, D. and Combs, A.W. *Individual Behavior.* New York: Harpers, 1949.
10. Maslow, A.H. See Reference 2, above.
11. Ellis, A. *Reason and Emotion in Psychotherapy.* Seacaucus, New Jersey: Lyle Stuart, 1962.
12. Ellis, A. Rational-Emotive Therapy, in Corsini, R.J. (Editor), *Current Psychotherapies.* Itasca, Illinois: Peacock, 1973, page 167.
13. Beck, A.T. *Cognitive Therapies and the Emotional Disorders.* New York: International Universities Press, 1976.
14. Bandura, A. Self-Efficacy: Toward a Unifying Theory of Behavior Change, *Psychological Review,* 1977, 89, 191-215.
15. Meichenbaum, D., See Reference 22, Chapter 3.
16. Foureyt, J.P. and Goodrick, G.K. Cognitive Behavior Therapy, in R.J. Corsini, See Reference 5, above.
17. Phillips, E.L., See Reference 5, Chapter 3.
18. Foureyt, J.P., et al., See Reference 16, above.

Chapter 5
The Newer Psychotherapies & Auxiliary Therapies

1. Herink, R. (Editor). *The Psychotherapy Handbook: The A to Z Guide to More Than 250 Different Therapies in Use Today.* New York: The New American Library, Inc., 1980. Corsini, R.J. *Current Psychotherapies,* See Reference 12, Chapter 4. Patterson, C.H. *Relationship, Counseling and Psychotherapy.* New York: Harper & Row, 1974. Rosenbaum, M. (Editor). *Handbook of Short-Term Therapy Groups.* New York: McGraw-Hill, 1984.
2. Harper, R.A. *Psychoanalysis & Psychotherapy.* Inglewood Cliffs, New Jersey: Prentice-Hall, 1959. Harper, R.A. *The New Psychotherapies.* New York: Prentice-Hall, 1975.
3. Corsini, R.J., See Reference 5, Chapter 4.
4. Corsini, R.J., See Reference 5, Chapter 4.
5. Brown, G., McDowell, R.L. and Smith, J. *Educating Adolescents with Behavior Disorders.* Columbus, Ohio: Charles E. Merrill, 1981.
6. Brown, G., et al., See Reference 5, above.
7. Phillips, E.L. Conflict Resolution Therapy, in Corsini, R.J. (Editor). See Reference 5, Chapter 4.
8. Phillips, E.L., See Reference 6, Introduction.
9. Schwartz, M.D. *Using Computers in Clinical Practice: Psychotherapy and Mental Health Applications.* New York: Haworth, 1984.
10. *Standards for Educational and Psychological Tests.* Washington, D.C., American Psychological Association, 1974.

11. Schwartz, M.D., See Reference 9, above.
12. Reynolds, D.K. *Morita Therapy.* Berkeley: University of California Press, 1976. Reynolds, D.K. *The Quiet Therapies.* Honolulu: University of Hawaii Press, 1980. Reynolds, D.K. *Naikan Therapy: Meditation for Self Development in Japan.* Chicago: University of Chicago Press, 1983.
13. Reynolds, D.K., See Reference 12, above (1980).
14. Reynolds, D.K., See Reference 12, above (1980).
15. Reynolds, D.K., See Reference 12, above (1980).
16. Reynolds, D.K., See Reference 12, above (1980).
17. Kupers, T.A. *Public Therapy: The Practice of Psychotherapy In The Public Mental Health Clinic.* New York: Free Press, 1981.

Chapter 6
Self-Help and Support Groups

1. Levy, L.H., Self-Help Groups: Types and Psychological Processes. *Journal of Applied Behavioral Science.* 1976, 12, 310-322.
2. Weber, G.H. and Cohen, L.M., *Beliefs and Self-Help.* New York: Human Sciences Press, 1982.
3. Veroff, J.B., Kulka, R.A. and Douvan, E. *Mental Health in America: Patterns of Help Seeking from 1957 to 1976.* New York: Basic Books, 1981.
4. Stokes, B., *Helping Ourselves: Local Solutions to Global Problems.* New York: Norton, 1981.
5. Rodin, M.B., Community Organization and Self-Help. In Weber, G.H. and Cohen, L.M., See Reference 2, above.
6. Gross, M.L., *The Psychological Society.* New York: Random House, 1978. Chu, F.D., and Trotter, S. *The Madness Establishment: Ralph Nadar's Study Group Report on the National Institute of Mental Health.* New York: Grossman, 1974. Zilbergeld, B. *The Shrinking of America: Myths of Psychological Change.* New York: Little, Brown & Co., 1983. Maguire, L. *Understanding Social Networks.* Beverly Hills: Sage Publications, 1983. Leavitt, J.W. (Ed.) *Women and Health in America.* Madison: University of Wisconsin Press, 1984. Veroff, J., et al., See Reference 3, above. Yates, B.T., *Self-Management.* Belmont, CA: Wadsworth, 1985.
7. Maguire, L., See Reference 6, above.
8. Kiesler, C.A., Cummings, N.A., & VandenBos, G.R. *Psychology and National Health Insurance: A Source Book.* Washington, D.C.: American Psychological Association, 1979.
9. Cummings, N.A., Follette, W.T., Brief Therapy and Medical Utilization: An 8-Year Follow-Up. In Dorken, et al., *Professional Psychology Today.* San Francisco: Jossey Bass, 1976. Follette, W.T. and Cummings, N.A. Psychiatric Services and Medical Utilization in a Prepaid Health Setting, *Medical Care,* 1967, 5, 25-35.
10. Sifneos, P.E. *Short-Term Psychotherapy and Emotional Crisis.* Cambridge: Harvard University Press, 1972. Mann, J. *Time-Limited Psychotherapy.* Cambridge: Harvard University Press, 1973. Wolberg, L.R. *Handbook of Short-Term Psychotherapy.* New York: Thiene-Stratton, 1980.
11. Comstock, C.H., Preventative Processes in Self-Help Groups: Parents Anonymous. In Borman, L.D., Borck, L.E., Hess, R., and Pasquale, F.L. (Eds.) *Helping People to Help Themselves.* New York: Haworth Press, 1982.
12. Gottleib, B.H. (Ed.), *Social Networks and Social Support.* Beverly Hills: Sage Publications, 1981. Gartner, A. and Reissman, F. *Self-Help and the Human Services.* San Francisco: Jossey-Bass, 1977.
13. Korchin, S.J., *Modern Clinical Psychology.* New York: Basic Books, 1976.
14. Borman, L.D., See Reference 11, above.

Chapter 7
Intercultural and Other Cultural Therapies

1. Phillips, E.L., See Reference 5, Chapter 3.
2. Parloff, M.B., Waskow, I.F., and Wolfe, B.F. Research on Therapist Variables in Relation to Process and Outcome. In S.L. Garfield and A.F. Bergin (Eds.) *Handbook of Psychotherapy and Behavior Change.* New York: Wiley, 1978, 2nd Ed.
3. Hollingshead, A.B., and Redlich, F.C. *Social Class and Mental Illness: A Community Study.* New York: Wiley, 1958.
4. Abt, L.E., and Stuart, I.R. (Eds.), *The Newer Therapies: A Source Book.* New York; Van Nostrand Reinhold, 1982. Schofield, J.W., *Black and White In School: Trust, Tension or Tolerance.* New York: Praeger, 1982.
5. Eron, L.D. and Peterson, R.A., Abnormal Behavior: Social Approaches, *Annual Review of Psychology,* 1982, 33, 245-252.
6. Triandis, H.C., and Draguns, J.G., (Eds.), *Handbook of Cross-Cultural Psychology: Psychopathology,* Vol. 6, Boston: Allyn and Bacon, 1980.
7. Frank, J.F. *Persuasion and Healing.* Balti: Johns-Hopkins University Press, 1973. 2nd Ed.
8. Tseng, W.S. and Hsu, J., Cultural and Psychotherapy. In A.J. Marsalla, R.G. Tharp, and T.J. Ciborowski, (Eds.), *Perspectives on Cross-Cultural Psychology.* New York: Academic Press, 1979. Adler, L.L. (Ed.), *Cross-Cultural Research at Issue.* New York: Academic Press, 1982. (Especially chapters 24-29, inclusively.)
9. Katz, M.M., Cole, J.O. and Lowery, H.A. Studies of the Diagnostic Process: The Influence of Symptom, Perception, Past Experience, and Ethnic Background on Diagnostic Decisions, *American Journal of Psychiatry,* 1969, 125, 109-119.
10. van der Hart, O. *Rituals in Psychotherapy: Transition and Continuity.* New York: Irvington, 1983.
11. Reynolds, D.R., See Reference 12, Chapter 5.

Chapter 8
Environmental Factors: The Neglected Perspective

1. Corsini, R.J., See Reference 5, Chapter 4.
2. Kendler, H.H., *Psychology: A Science in Conflict.* New York: Oxford University Press, 1981.
3. Phillips, E.L. and Wiener, D.N., See Reference 4, Introduction.
4. Zussman, M. You: The Frustration Factor. Washington POST, August 31, 1984, pg. B-5.

Chapter 9
Taking Over for Yourself
(And Who Needs More Than Short-Term Help?)

1. Back, K.W., *Beyond Words: The Story of Sensitivity Training and the Encounter Movement.* New York: Russell Sage Foundation, 1972.
2. Chassick, R.C., *Why Psychotherapists Fail.* New York: Aronson, 1971.
3. Silverman, L.H., Frank, S.G., & Dachinger, P., A Psychoanalytic Reinterpretation of the Effectiveness of Systematic Sensitization: Experimental Data Bearing on the Role of Merging Fantasies, *Journal of Abnormal Psychology,* 1974, 83, 313-318.
4. Emmelkamp, P.M.G., *Phobic and Obsessive-Compulsive Disorders: Theory, Research, and Practice.* New York: Plenum, 1982. Beech, H.R., and Vaughan, M., *Behavioral Treatment of Obsessional States.* New York: Wiley, 1978.

Chapter 10
Beyond Therapy

1. Gross, M.L., *The Psychological Society.* New York: Simon & Schuster, 1978.
2. Eysenck, H.J., *The Effects of Psychotherapy.* New York: International Science Press, 1966.
3. Tennov, D., See Reference 7, Chapter 3.
4. Garfield, S.L., See Reference 8, Chapter 3.
5. Zilbergeld, B., See Reference 1, Chapter 3.
6. Herink, R., See Reference 1, Chapter 5.
7. Phillips, E.L., *Stress, Health, and Psychological Problems in the Major Professions.* Lanham, MD: University Press of America, 1982.
8. Kendler, H.H., See Reference 2, Chapter 8.
9. Garfield, S.A., and Kurz, M., Evaluation of Treatment and Related Procedures in 1216 Cases Referred to Mental Hygiene Clinics, *Psychiatric Quarterly,* 1952, 26, 414-424.
10. Phillips, E.L., See Reference 5, Chapter 3.
11. Parloff, et al., Page 11, See Reference 2, Chapter 7.
12. Bloom, B.L., Focused Single-Session Therapy: Initial Development and Evaluation. In Budman, *Forms of Brief Therapy.* New York: Guilford, 1981, page 172.
13. Smith, M.L., Glass, G.V., & Miller, T.I., *The Benefits of Psychotherapy,* Baltimore: Johns-Hopkins University Press, 1980.
14. Gallo, B.S., Meta-Analysis — A Mixed Meta-Phor, *American Psychologist,* 1978, 33, 515-517.

INDEX

T

U

V

W

Y

Z